THE LIFE AND DEATH OF AN ICONIC
MOUNTAIN COMMUNITY

Daniel S. Pierce

Great Smoky Mountains Association
Gatlinburg, Tennessee

Published by Great Smoky Mountains Association, a private, nonprofit organization
which supports the educational, scientific, and historical programs of Great Smoky
Mountains National Park. Our publications are an educational service intended to en-
hance the public's understanding and enjoyment of the national park. If you would like to
know more about our publications, memberships, guided hikes and other projects please
contact:

Great Smoky Mountains Association
P. O. Box 130
Gatlinburg,Tennessee
(865) 436-7318
www.SmokiesInformation.org

ISBN # 978-0-937207-85-7

Edited by Steve Kemp and Kent Cave
Book Design and Illustration by Joey Heath
Historic photographs courtesy: National Park Service Archives and D. H. Ramsey Library
Special Collections, UNC 28804
Cover Photo: Josh Calhoun home, Bone Valley
Editorial Assistance by Julie Brown and Cyn Slaughter
01 02 03 04 05 06 07 08 09 10

To Lydia, my love, my mountain muse.

Contents

Introduction

It has never been easy to get to Hazel Creek, not 6,000 years ago when humans first came to the area, not today. The name Hazel Creek belies the title of "creek" as it is wider than many so-called rivers in the region for much of its length. Its 15-mile course, with a watershed also as wide at its apex, has amazing biodiversity and reportedly contains nearly every plant known to Great Smoky Mountains National Park. It also teems with wildlife and has one of the densest populations of black bears and wild hogs in the region. I once saw a grouse as big as a chicken calmly strolling down the middle of the trail in Proctor and walks along the trail are often punctuated by the jungle-like calls of Pileated Woodpeckers. The scenery in the watershed varies from pine-clad lakeside coves, to sycamore-lined stream on the lower reaches of the creek, to increasingly boulder-strewn courses as the elevation rises, to waterfalls in high-elevation spruce-fir forests, all the way to the crest of the Smokies on the North Carolina/Tennessee state line and the expansive views looking down into Cades Cove from the ridgetop.

The early Native Americans who came to Hazel Creek followed game trails on foot or perhaps took their canoes hewed from giant tuliptrees down the Little Tennessee River to the creek's mouth. Early European-American settlers followed those same rugged trails but did have the added convenience of horses or mules to ride and carry in supplies. Horace Kephart famously arrived on Hazel Creek in 1904 in a horse-drawn wagon driven by Granville Calhoun, picked up at the train station at Bushnell. I won't wade into the controversy over Kephart's state of mind, health, or level of sobriety when he came to the area, but his getting to Hazel Creek was facilitated by the relatively recent arrival of the Southern Railroad to the neighborhood and a road built to haul copper ore out of mines up on the Little Fork of Sugar Fork, a Hazel Creek tributary.

Access to Hazel Creek was probably at its easiest later in the first decade of the 20th century when the Southern Railroad extended its line to the mouth of Hazel Creek and Ritter Lumber Company built a railroad to its mill at Proctor, a few miles up the creek, and narrow gauge lines into the upper reaches of the watershed. By the 1910s, a person could jump on a logging train at Walkers Creek, change to a passenger train in Proctor, do some shopping in Bryson City and be back home for dinner if you could make all your train connections. Access improved even more with the construction of NC Highway 288 in 1928. From then until 1944, you could actually drive an automobile (barring high water) into Hazel Creek, although the phrase "long and winding road" took on literal meaning in this case.

When the Tennessee Valley Authority closed the flood gates of Fontana Dam in 1944, access to Hazel Creek reverted to hiking and horse trails, many following those ancient Native American paths, and a long trek. With Fontana Lake now coming up to the edge of the former town of Proctor, you can also take a canoe, kayak, or motorboat across from the Fontana Marina or from the Cable Cove U.S. Forest Service boat ramp. The most convenient way to get there is to take the daily boat shuttle from Fontana Marina. Even with modern boat access, however, it still requires planning and a good bit of time, if not physical effort, to get to Hazel Creek.

My first trip into Hazel Creek involved a more ancient mode of transport than Granville Calhoun's horse-drawn wagon; a canoe, albeit one made of fiberglass, not carved from a tuliptree in the Cherokee style. My older brother David, an inveterate outdoorsman and locally famous trout fisherman, and I, like Kephart, sought a "Back of Beyond" to experience the "joys of the chase" for Hazel Creek's legendary rainbow, brown, and native speckled trout. My usual trout fishing luck held and I got "nary a bite," but I soon came to appreciate the natural attractions of Hazel Creek and its watershed and the challenges of getting there.

As I've found in my own path to doing research on this place, it is also difficult to "get to Hazel Creek," to understand the place in the metaphorical sense. The Hazel Creek watershed is by no means the largest in the Great Smoky Mountains and while beautiful and rich with botanical and zoological life, is no more beautiful or rich in life than other Smokies watersheds. Despite being such a seemingly unexceptional place on the surface, Hazel Creek is a place that has fascinated, mystified, and invoked intense passion in people in a manner that the nearby watersheds of Forney, Noland, Eagle, Twenty-Mile, Deep, and even Cataloochee creeks have not. Indeed, only Cades Cove, a much more accessible spot and one of the most visited sites in the region, engenders more attention and perhaps as much mystique. It is not easy to grasp why Hazel Creek has such a powerful hold on so many people when it is so hard to visit and relatively few people living today have actually been there.

That is what this book is about; a perhaps feeble attempt at explaining what makes this place so special. The answer to that question, however, is not simple as Hazel Creek means, and has meant over the years, many things to many people. For Native Americans, early settlers, and 20th century hunters and fishermen, Hazel Creek provided a rich place for gathering nuts, berries, and medicinal herbs, a place that produced big bear for the hunt, and plentiful fish in its streams. It meant a home place for a hardy group of early settlers like Moses Proctor who came into the watershed seeking cheap land for subsistence farms, plentiful grazing land in the nearby mountains for their hogs and cattle, and who did not mind, and perhaps welcomed, the remoteness of the site. After the Civil War, moonshiners, like Quill Rose from nearby Eagle Creek, definitely welcomed the isolation of the area and their ability to shield their operations from prying eyes and easily shift between North Carolina and Tennessee to avoid capture by revenue agents.

Outdoorsman and author Horace Kephart, the Hazel Creek watershed's most famous resident, came to the area in 1904 seeking a "Back of Beyond," a place where he could "enjoy a free life in the open air, the thrill of exploring new ground, the joys of the chase, and the man's game of matching my wood-craft against the forces of nature . . ." Kephart found the open spaces he sought, but it was his observations of his neighbors in the area, accurate or not, that his readers most remembered. His stories secured a spot for Hazel Creek and its people in the nation's popular imagination. Kephart's writings also provided generations of Americans with an image of Hazel Creek, and the entire southern Appalachian region, as a "strange land" peopled by moonshiners and bear hunters tilling and living on "perpendicular fields" much the same way as their ancestors in the British Isles lived in the 16th century.

For most area residents in the late 19th and early 20th centuries, however, living on Hazel Creek did not mean the preservation of the language, economic life, or folkways of Elizabethan England or being isolated from the currents of American progress, but the embracing of the modern industrial world. That world physically, mentally, economically, socially, and spiritually transformed the watershed with its dramatic boom and bust cycles. Residents and the many newcomers who came to the area to take advantage of the employment opportunities in the copper mines and timber camps that cropped up seemingly overnight rode the waves of previously unimaginable prosperity followed by periods where the mines closed and the timber companies moved on and those waves crashed down wreaking havoc throughout the community. Despite the whiplash effect of modern life, Hazel Creekers picked themselves up, made do with what they had and could scrape together and hoped a new lifting industrial wave would come along.

The last period of industrial era boom and bust came with the construction of the Fontana Dam, the dramatic and painful removal of all the human residents of Hazel Creek, and the dismantling or outright destruction of their homes, schools, churches, and businesses. Overnight, this watershed which had recently been the home of thousands of people, became a place whose only permanent human residents were those individuals interred in the cemeteries scattered along the hillsides.

Interestingly, this period when Hazel Creek became de-populated helped to produce a passionate and intense attachment to the place among the former residents who were removed and among many of their descendants. Nostalgic stories of life on Hazel Creek became common in books, newspaper articles, newsletters, and oral history collections in the region. The emotional attachment to Hazel Creek only grew more intense as community memories became intertwined in a powerful way with the preservation, care, and decoration of cemeteries and to the unfulfilled promise of the federal government to build a new road into the area, a road that would not only provide access to the cemeteries, but might promote a tourism boom that would benefit the struggling rural economy of Swain and neighboring counties.

As building foundations, left-behind logging and mining equipment, and even the rusting remains of abandoned automobiles became increasingly obscured by underbrush and as the forest began to recover from the onslaught of industrial logging, Hazel Creek became once again a kind of "Back of Beyond." As such it became another very modern thing, a human-created wilderness where active management by the National Park Service attempted to eliminate much of the evidence of human habitation and use in the area. This management style was welcomed by increasing numbers of wilderness seekers from the 1960s on as backpackers sought a relatively easy trip into the solitude of the backcountry and fly fishermen sought big brown and rainbow trout on Hazel Creek and its tributaries. Articles in magazines promoting both adventures in the wilderness and adventures for fly fishermen extolled Hazel Creek as a place to escape the modern world and all vestiges of human impact.

While perhaps there were some skirmishes on Hazel Creek among Indians over the millennia before Europeans came and numbers of 19th and 20th century residents went off to battle in faraway places from the Civil War to World War II, historically Hazel Creek was a relatively peaceful and neighborly place with only the occasional outburst of violence or even major disagreement. For much of the last 40 years, however, Hazel Creek has been known far and wide as a battleground, not one involving physical violence, but a battleground between passionate "build the road" advocates, most of whom lived locally or had strong local ties, who demanded the federal government fulfill its promises, and equally passionate wilderness advocates, many from far away, who demanded that the government protect the area "unimpaired for future generations."

While the road issue has been partially resolved and most people believe a new road into Hazel Creek will never be built, Hazel Creek remains a place whose legacy is often disputed. As an author and researcher looking at this place, I'm not here to settle any disputes or even to take any sides. My hope is that this look at the complex history of a place that has invoked such love and passion will help inform future debates among those who care so much about it. As Hazel Creek fades from the news headlines, I also hope this book will expose increasing numbers of people to the fascinating and complex story of a relatively small place with a huge history.

Acknowledgments and Notes on Sources

Sometimes you realize well after you've agreed to do something, exactly what you've actually gotten yourself into. Such was the case when I agreed to do a little book on Hazel Creek and its human history for the fine folks at the Great Smoky Mountains Association. Very quickly I realized I would be retracing the footsteps of the many talented writers and historians who have visited, lived in, done research, and written about this place. I'll forever be indebted to writers and researchers like Wilbur Ziegler, Ben Grosscup, Grace Lumpkin, Samuel Hunnicutt, Jim Gasque, Bob Plott, Don Kirk, Harry Middleton, Alan and Karen Jabbour, Lance Holland, and David Monteith. It was especially gratifying to be reminded of what a talented and insightful historian my old graduate school friend Stephen Taylor is when I repeatedly consulted his fine book *The New South's New Frontier.*

Of course, anyone who does research on Hazel Creek owes a particular debt of gratitude to three giants on whose shoulders I stand: Granville Calhoun, while never publishing any writings, gave countless interviews chronicling life on Hazel Creek from the 1880s to the 1940s; Horace Kephart, whose detailed, and yes controversial, observations provide rich detail of life on the creek in the early 20th century; and Duane Oliver whose *Hazel Creek Then and Now* combines sound scholarship, the oral traditions of the place, and Oliver's own deep personal experience.

I am also tremendously indebted to those who provided personal assistance in researching and writing this book. Steve Kemp of the Great Smoky Mountains Association first had the idea for the book and commissioned me to write it. Any credit for the look of this book goes to Steve and his talented staff who always seem to be able to transcend my poor efforts at writing and make me look good. Historians are always dependent on the skill and aid of archivists and this work greatly benefited from the help of Michael Aday at the Archives of Great Smoky Mountains National Park and from George Frizzell at Western Carolina University's Special Collections.

Jim Casada was both patient and insightful in helping me "wade through" the lore, legend, and fact of Hazel Creek's rich hunting and fishing history. George Ellison and Janet McCue provided invaluable assistance in evaluating Horace Kephart's experience and his writings on Hazel Creek. Bill Hart opened his personal archive to me and shared generously of his research and personal experience with the history of the Great Smoky Mountains. I was able to spend a wonderful day with Wendy Myers and Don Casada where they generously shared their exhaustive research on the North Shore area. I am especially indebted to Don who provided invaluable insight into the early settlement of the area, answered innumerable questions over email, and even took me on a tour of the Bryson City Cemetery which provided much of the basis for the conclusion to this book.

I must also thank the friends and family members who supported me through the process of researching and writing this book. I first experienced Hazel Creek with Richard Starnes and David Perry. While we never found the fly-fishing Eden that David swore lay just around the next bend of Bone Valley Creek, the experience helped spark my love for this place. My brother David Pierce supplied canoes, fly-fishing expertise, and wonderful company on several trips from the boat landing at Cable Cove to Hazel Creek. Bill and Lynn George and Evan Gurney helped me see Hazel Creek through fresh eyes when they accompanied David and me on trips across the lake. The enthusiastic love of nature, particularly of the Great Smoky Mountains, that all four of my children—Anna Clare, Taylor, Sully, and Coulter—display has helped fuel my own enthusiasm and I am always indebted to them for the inspiration they provide daily.

Finally, I must thank my wife Lydia to whom this book is dedicated. Practically since the day we met our relationship has revolved around our mutual love for nature. I feel so fortunate to have shared many of our most precious moments in 32 years of marriage with her enjoying the great outdoors, including time well spent on Hazel Creek. My career as a historian and writer would have been impossible without her unconditional love and support.

About the Author

Daniel S. Pierce is an avid hiker and biker who has spent almost 50 years of his life in western North Carolina. He is the author of *The Great Smokies: From Natural Habitat to National Park* (UT Press, 2000), *Real NASCAR: White Lightning, Red Clay, and Big Bill France* (UNC Press, 2010), and *Corn From a Jar: Moonshining in the Great Smoky Mountains* (GSMA, 2013) and serves as Professor of History, NEH Distinguished Professor in the Humanities, and resident professional hillbilly at the University of North Carolina-Asheville.

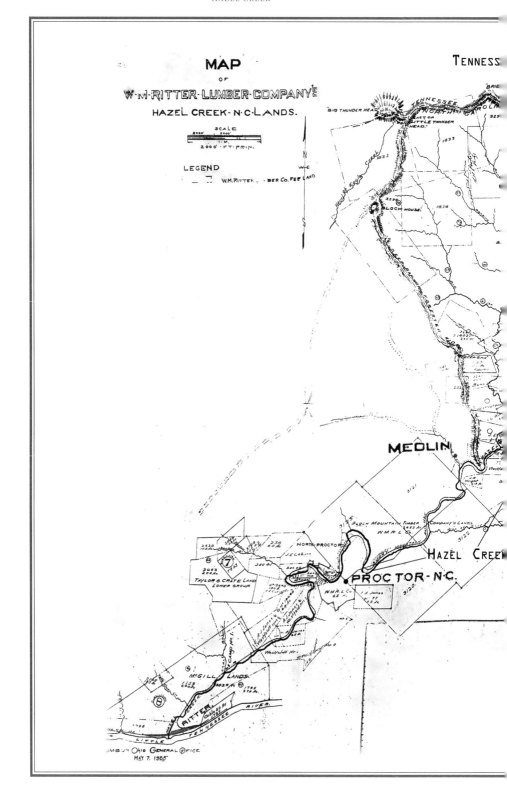

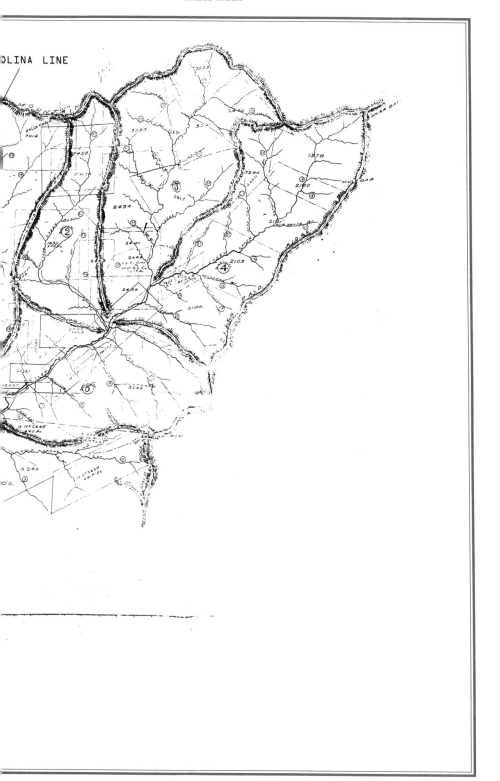

CHAPTER ONE

The First Arrivals

*T*oday the National Park Service manages the Hazel Creek watershed as a natural area where humans can visit but not remain. However, human activity has shaped the Hazel Creek watershed for at least 6,000 years. We do not know the names of the first peoples who inhabited the area during what archaeologists term the Archaic period, but from the evidence gathered by scholars, and by later residents digging up projectile points — or as they called them in Hazel Creek, "Indian heads" — in their fields and gardens, it appears as if ancient Native Americans used the area primarily for seasonal gathering and hunting trips.

The rich cornucopia of flora and fauna along the creek attracted these hunter-gatherers who set up seasonal camps at strategic points. In spring groups of women harvested the wild greens so important to boost the vitamin and mineral content after a long winter of primarily consuming dried foods. In summer groups gathered berries, grapes, herbs and plants like ginseng, pennyroyal, pink root, and snake-root that they employed for a variety of medicinal purposes. In fall these earliest inhabitants came to the Hazel Creek watershed for the hard mast: acorns, hickories, walnuts, and especially chestnuts that were so easily preserved and later eaten raw or turned into flour.

The natural botanical bounty of the area also made it an ideal site for seasonal hunts, particularly in late fall when sparse leaf cover made game easier to spot, deer became less cautious because of the rut, and as their hair and fur thickened. Bear have particularly thrived in the Hazel Creek watershed which still provides some of

Ayunini

THERE IS EVIDENCE OF INTERMITTENT NATIVE AMERICAN OCCUPATION IN THE HAZEL CREEK AREA. THE ARCHAEOLOGICAL RECORD TELLS US THAT THE WATERSHED HAS BEEN USED EXTENSIVELY BY INDIGENOUS PEOPLES FROM THE EARLY ARCHAIC PERIOD THROUGH INDIAN REMOVAL. HUNTING, GATHERING, AND THE ESTABLISHMENT OF AT LEAST SEASONAL CAMPS HAS TAKEN PLACE FOR MANY THOUSANDS OF YEARS THERE.

the finest bear habitat in the eastern United States. As author John Carter observed in *Trails of the Past*, "The whole area afforded one of the best feeding grounds that it has ever been my privilege to hunt in. Acorns, nuts, grapes, berries, and many other types of food were in abundance. Not only was food plentiful to support a large number of bear but the terrain was well adapted to the protection of the bear population."

Native American men used the same seasonal camps that women employed for gathering expeditions and spent weeks in communal hunts to secure enough meat to make it through the winter, along with hides and furs to help them weather the cold. While these Archaic Indians primarily consumed venison, they prized bear meat for its high fat content and used bear fat in salves and as fuel for lamps. Bones found in ancient trash heaps also reveal they consumed smaller game such as squirrels, rabbits, ground hogs, and turkeys that were also common to the area.

While there is limited evidence of more permanent settlements on Hazel Creek during the Archaic and subsequent Woodland periods, early Native Americans left a distinct imprint on the environment in important ways. Given their low population densities, their hunting and gathering activities had little major impact on the land, the flora, and the fauna, but the way they managed the land and resources through the use of fire shaped the landscape. Peat-bog studies conducted by ethnobotanists Paul and Hazel Delcourt in the lower Little Tennessee Valley near Franklin, North Carolina reveal a pattern of regular woods burning throughout the Archaic and Woodland periods. Native Americans used fire during these periods to clear camp sites of vegetation, insects, and snakes. They set fire to the forests to maintain more open vistas in order to better spot enemies and game. Such fires also promoted the sprouting of hardwoods; burned off leaf litter thereby making hard mast easier to find; created a favorable environment for fire-resistant trees such as chestnuts, a wide variety of oaks, walnuts, and hickories; and created ideal habitat for deer, turkeys, and bear.

There is at least some evidence that Native American use of fire played a role in the creation of one of the distinctive geographic feature of the southern Appalachian region, the grass bald. While it is unlikely Indians created these spaces themselves, it is a distinct possibility that they used fire to maintain balds created by natural forces, such as lightning fires and freezing and thawing, as game attractors. Cherokee legends, recorded by ethnologist James Mooney in the 1890s, lend some credence to the notion that at least some grass balds in the Smokies—particularly Gregory Bald, not far west of Hazel Creek—preceded European settlement. Known to the Cherokee as Tsistu'yi, or Rabbit Place, according to Cherokee lore Gregory Bald is the place where the Great Rabbit held council in his townhouse.

For the Cherokee and their predecessors, fire was a beneficent, even a sacred, force. According to Gary Godwin, "The Cherokees maintained a great reverence for fire, considering it equal to water in importance, the 'giver of good things,' and the focal point of power and life." As environmental historian Stephen Pyne put it, "Anthropogenic fire made the world more habitable for those who held the torch." And such behavior definitely shaped at least parts of the environment of the Hazel Creek watershed.

Some time in the last 1,000 years or so, a group of Native Americans who called themselves the Ani-Yun-Wiya, or the Principal People, arrived in the Hazel Creek area. We know them better as the Cherokee. The exact date of their arrival is unclear, but most academics believe they moved south from present day western New York due to their linguistic ties to the Iroquois Indian groups of that area. They brought with them, or adapted from Native Americans already living in the area, a way of life characterized as Mississippian, a life that added the cultivation of domesticated plants to hunting and gathering practices of the Archaic and Woodland periods. For the Cherokee, the cultivation of the sacred Three Sisters—maize (corn), beans, and squashes—became as important as deer, bear, ginseng, and chestnuts to both diet and culture. This dietary diversity sparked a growth in population, allowed for a richer cultural life, and promoted a lifestyle centered on fixed village sites.

This move toward "fixity," did not, however, dramatically change the way that Native Americans used the Hazel Creek area. Archaeological evidence suggests that while there may have been a few scattered sites where Cherokee conducted agriculture along the lower reaches of the creek, for the most part they followed the pattern of the Archaic and Woodland Indians coming to the area seasonally for hunting and gathering activities. Not surprisingly, the scattered sites where the Cherokee had burned off bottom land for agriculture became the "old fields" that early Euro-Americans first settled on when they arrived in the late 1820s.

While a relatively isolated place, Hazel Creek was connected to the broader Cherokee and Native American world by several well-worn trails. Trails inter-connecting the Cherokee "mother town" of Kituwah, the Middle Towns near present-day Franklin, North Carolina, the Valley Towns on the Valley River near present-day Andrews, and the Overhill Towns clustered near the confluence of the Little Tennessee and Tennessee Rivers, ran along the Little Tennessee River and crossed the mouth of Hazel Creek. Another well-traveled trail connected Cades Cove and Hazel Creek. The route ran out of the Cove along Forge Creek to Ekaneetlee Branch, through Ekaneetlee Gap, down Ekaneetlee Creek to Eagle Creek, then over Soapstone Gap to Possum Hollow. This trail was especially important to the Cherokee as it provided access to an outcropping of soapstone used for pipes and other ceremonial and utilitarian objects.

The Cherokee tried to hold off encroachment by the British and then the United States, but gradual cessions of land opened the Great Smoky Mountains, including Hazel Creek, to white settlement. In 1819 the Cherokee ceded the land north of the Little Tennessee River by treaty to the United States. Given its relative remoteness and the availability of plenty of land near more accessible areas, interest

THE SACRED THREE SISTERS, MAIZE, BEANS AND SQUASH—
ENABLED NATIVE AMERICANS TO ESTABLISH MORE FIXED
HOMESITES AND VILLAGES IN THE MOUNTAIN REGION.

and settlement in Hazel Creek proceeded slowly. Land titles during this period are murky at best, but land speculators purchased most of the Hazel Creek area during the 1850s and '60s. Historian Stephen Taylor observed that, "… much of the lowest-quality land [which would have included most of Hazel Creek] was bought by land speculators or remained unsold." Further complicating the issue, Taylor also noted that, "… the hilly tracts tended to change hands frequently." Recent research by Don Casada in the North Carolina State Archives and the state's MARS online catalog reveal sizable land grants of 640 acres or more in the area to Ephraim Ammons in 1838, Silas McDowell in 1854, Samuel Sherrill and George and R.N. Wikle in 1855, J. R. Siler and A. Brooks in 1857, C. L. Walker in 1862, E. B. Olmsted in 1867, and Phillip Jenkins in 1869. Although called grants, these were lands purchased from the state probably for ten cents or less per acre.

Surprisingly, the first white settlers who came into Hazel Creek did not travel west from settlements in western North Carolina, but over the Smokies from Cades Cove. Moses Proctor, his wife Patience, and son William traveled the Cherokee trail once used to access soapstone deposits to cross the mountains and settle in what became known as Possum Hollow, according to Duane Oliver, "a little before 1830." Proctor probably squatted on the land, but given the isolation of the place it was unlikely that the State of North Carolina would even know he was there much less try to evict him from the property. Proctor evidently liked the place, even its isolation, built his cabin, and settled in. The family grew with the birth of another son Hiram in 1832 and a daughter Catherine in 1837. Moses Proctor's son James did enter a claim to 100 acres of state land in 1854 but a deed was not registered, and therefore the land was not legally theirs, until 1863. Moses Proctor did buy 50 acres of land on Hazel Creek in 1860 for $10 from Fonz Marcus of Cherokee County.

Proctor's arrival did not set off a land rush by any means as additional settlers came in at a slow trickle. In 1835, Samuel Cable tripled the population of the Hazel Creek area when he, his wife Elizabeth, and seven children followed the trail from Cades Cove and settled further down the creek at its confluence with what became known as Cable Branch. The Cables seemed to follow the same casual arrangement to registering their claims with the state as the Proctors. They did enter claims to state land but not until the late 1840s and early 1850s. However, deeds on these properties were not issued until the 1870s. It took a marriage between Catherine Proctor and Joseph Welch of nearby Forney Creek to bring the next homeowners. Welch filed for two 50-acre land grants from the state in 1849 and the deeds to the property were not registered until 1854 and 1859. Josiah and Sarah Bradshaw soon joined them. The Proctors, Cables, Welches, and Bradshaws and their descendants formed the backbone of the Hazel Creek community for the next 90-plus years.

Stories passed down over the years by these earliest white settlers recall that there were still a few Cherokee living in the area even after forced removal and the Trail of Tears in the late 1830s. Catherine Proctor recounted several instances of contact with Cherokee neighbors, but it appears that most of the local Native Americans did not interact a great deal with the white families on Hazel Creek. Duane Oliver does recount the story of Hezekiah Jones developing a close relationship to a Cherokee family in the 1860s. Stories of Cherokee living on, or near, the creek persisted into that period but the remnants of the never large Native American population seem to have moved away, probably east to the Qualla Boundary in Jackson County or west to the Snowbird community in Graham County.

Life for those early white settlers on Hazel Creek did not differ appreciably from the Cherokee who preceded them on the land and focused primarily on basic subsistence. All of them grew large crops of corn in the creek bottoms as the staple of life, most of which they ground into meal in small turbine mills, or tub mills, located on local creeks. Anna Elizabeth recalled the manner in which families sorted and graded their corn: "The best corn was saved for seed. The middle-grade corn was for grinding into cornmeal & for making hominy; the rest was for feeding the milk cows & hogs."

Hazel Creek farmers also grew a variety of other crops including the other two sisters; beans, such as greasy cutshorts and leather-britches, and several types of squashes, melons, and gourds, which had a variety of utilitarian purposes. Potatoes, turnips, carrots, and cabbages were also important because farm families easily stored them in a hole in the ground lined with straw, or, for more prosperous farmers, in a root cellar. Women had the task of preserving and pickling beans, cabbages, and peppers to help families survive the tough winter months. Elizabeth recalled that every year her mother put up "a fifty-gallon barrel of kraut & [a] fifty-gallon barrel of pickled green beans." Moses Proctor planted a peach orchard around 1840 and practically everyone planted apple trees, as Duane Oliver recounted, "the un-improved old varieties such as Buff, June, Sheepnose, Pippin, Limbertwig and La-dyskin…" Sorghum was another important farm product made into one of the few available sweeteners, molasses. Elizabeth's family made 100 gallons of molasses each year. She described the process: "When the cane was ready, the leaves were stripped off & saved for the livestock. Then the heads were cut off; next, the stalks were cut & laid in piles." Farmers then ran the cane between metal rollers turned by a mule or ox to squeeze the juice out, which they then cooked, stirred, and skimmed in large, flat pans until it reached the proper consistency.

The settlers also took advantage of the natural bounty around them and, like the Cherokee, actively participated in seasonal gathering. Women eagerly anticipated the spring green season and made big pots of wild lettuce, wild mustard, and poke greens cooked for hours with pork fatback. They also drank the "pot likker" where most of the vitamins and minerals ended up, a godsend after a winter poor in such necessities. Those early settlers also eagerly anticipated berry seasons which meant strawberry, blackberry, and blueberry pies as well as preserves and jellies. Fall meant chestnut season and a time for roasting and drying the oil-rich nuts for

Two Cherokee women

CHEROKEE WOMEN PASSED ALONG THEIR KNOWLEDGE OF MEDICINAL
HERBS FOUND IN THE HAZEL CREEK WATERSHED TO WHITE SETTLERS.

immediate consumption and for storage to tide folks through the long winters. Women also gathered many of the same medicinal herbs traditionally used by the Cherokee including black snakeroot, pink root, pennyroyal, spignet, tansy, boneset, sassafras, ragweed, and bloodroot. The one book that most folks in the area had on-hand, in addition to the Holy Bible, was *Gunn's Domestic Medicine*, a popular guide to medicinal herbs found in the mountain region, and other (supposed) curatives like mercury.

Men further supplemented the family diet by hunting in the mountains and fishing the many streams in the Hazel Creek watershed. They took to the woods with their rifles and shotguns individually to take small game such as squirrels, rabbits, and even groundhogs, and in hunts, using dogs, for deer and bear. Bear hunts became especially important communal events for men on Hazel Creek and over the years the community produced a number of legendary bear hunters and bear dogs. Fishing also became a favored pastime, in addition to being an important seasonal subsistence activity. Men would take to the streams and, in an era long before creel limits, pull out hundreds of small, but tasty native speckled trout. As Granville Calhoun recalled: "Why a man could catch a dishpan-full out of one pool in no time. They were so thick you could most knock 'em out of the water with a paddle." This usually led to another popular communal event, the fish fry.

The prime difference between the lifestyle of those early Hazel Creekers of European descent as opposed to their Cherokee counterparts was the significance of domestic animals. All of the families in the area possessed sizable herds of hogs and cattle. The hog served as one of the staples of life in Hazel Creek's "hog and hominy" lifestyle. These were not the domestic hogs we see in modern life, but feral animals who free-ranged the forest and ably fended for themselves. Horace Kephart colorfully described the hogs he encountered on Hazel Creek when he first arrived there in the early years of the 20th century: "Shaped in front like a thin wedge, he can go through laurel thickets like a bear. Armored with tough hide cushioned by bristles, he despises thorns, brambles and rattlesnakes, alike. His extravagantly long snout can scent like a cat's, and yet burrow, uproot, overturn, as if made of metal. The long legs, thin flanks, pliant hoofs, fit him to run like a deer and climb like a goat. In courage and sagacity he outranks all other beasts. A warrior born, he is also a strategist of the first order."

Indeed, hogs were the ideal source of protein for mountain communities like Hazel Creek as they required little tending, other than branding or marking of the young and castration of males, grew rapidly to maturity, reproduced prolifically, and yielded tasty and easily preserved meat. Kephart also praised the hog for these qualities: "The wild pig, roaming foot-loose and free over hill and dale, picks up his own living at all seasons and requires no attention at all [a slight exaggeration]. He is the cheapest possible source of meat and yields the quickest return…"

For the people of Hazel Creek, one of the most important annual communal events was the hog killing. The men culled young hogs from the herd, penned them, and fattened them up on corn in early fall. When the first frosts came, neighbors gathered at friends' farms to slaughter the animals and process the meat. The men dispatched the hogs with either a blow or shot to the head—often a rite of passage for boys—hung up the carcass to drain the blood, then dipped it in scalding water to make it easy to scrape the hair from the hide. No part of the hog went to waste. Entrails and organs were washed to be consumed fresh as delicacies, ground with meat for sausage, and used for sausage casings. The women turned skin into cracklins, rendered fat into lard, and turned brains and head meat into head cheese. Men cut the meat into manageable loins, hams, and shoulders, salted them down, and cured them in smoke houses.

Although as isolated as any community in the eastern United States, the folks on Hazel Creek also participated in the market economy and cattle were the key to that participation. Ironically, and primarily due to difficulties of preservation in a pre-refrigeration era, folks in the region rarely ate beef. While some kept a milk cow near their home, the primary reason they kept cattle was as a trade commodity, their primary source of cash. The people of Hazel Creek followed an ancient pattern of upland grazing where they drove their cattle to the high mountains in late spring, in the case of Hazel Creek, up the creek to Silers Bald on the state line. When that mountain became bald no one really knows, but Hazel Creek settlers undoubtedly expanded the bald area by both burning and grazing.

Once the men got the cattle to the mountains they turned them loose to graze and intermingle, with Hazel Creek cattle often grazing next to cattle owned by Cades Cove cousins. A few young men from the community spent their summers in small herders' cabins, the one most mentioned in Hazel Creek lore built by Crate Hall. By the late 19th century, Granville Calhoun estimated that Hazel Creek and Cades Cove farmers grazed at least 1,600 head of cattle on the balds of the western Smokies from Silers Bald to Gregory Bald.

In the fall, the men returned to the uplands, rounded up their cattle, and drove them back down the mountain. Hazel Creek farmers then sold off their yearling steers to drovers or drove them to market themselves. Most commonly they headed for East Tennessee where they sold the cattle for the cash needed to pay taxes or bartered for trade goods. Cattle were driven to market over drover roads that followed the ancient Indian paths. One of the reasons, perhaps, that Moses Proctor and others moved to Hazel Creek was its proximity to the Parsons Turnpike built in 1829. The turnpike ran from Chilhowee, Tennessee to Deals Gap on the state line, and a cattle trail followed the Little Tennessee River connecting it to Hazel Creek.

In the earliest days of the turnpike, the toll-keeper was mountain legend Nate Burchfield. According to journalist John Parris, Burchfield "was a giant of a man. He stood six-and-a-half feet tall, lean, sinewy, strong as a hickory. He was part Cherokee and his black hair fell to his shoulder." In exchange for maintaining the road, Burchfield, and his successors, collected tolls for wagons, horse and rider, and for each head of livestock. The earliest recorded tolls are from the early 20th century when toll keepers collected 10 cents per horse and rider, 15 to 25 cents per wagon (depending on the size of the load), and 3 cents per head of cattle. The Parsons Turnpike provided access to the booming cattle markets of Maryville and even Knoxville, which the railroad reached in 1855.

Less commonly, drovers took Hazel Creek cattle, hogs, and even turkeys east to markets in South Carolina and Georgia. After 1889, when the railroad reached nearby Bushnell on the Little Tennessee River, sending cattle east became much more common and market relationships with the rest of western North Carolina strengthened.

The importance of cattle to the Hazel Creek area is memorialized in the name of one of the creek's largest tributaries; Bone Valley Creek. The valley, and creek, received its name after a blizzard and intense cold snap trapped a herd of cattle on its upper reaches some time in the late 19th century. For years, the bleached bones of the unfortunate herd littered the valley floor, giving the area its eerie name.

While cattle were the most important trade commodity for folks on Hazel Creek in the 19th century, farmers in the area participated in a variety of other market activities. The gathering of medicinal herbs like pennyroyal, spignet, bloodroot, pink root, and black snakeroot brought cash or store credit from area storekeepers. Merchants like William Holland Thomas, who had one of his seven western North Carolina stores at nearby Cheoah, paid top prices for ginseng which found its way from Hazel Creek to Philadelphia and eventually to China. On the rare long trips to stores in East Tennessee or western North Carolina, Hazel Creekers also bartered for goods they could not produce themselves such as coffee, sugar, cloth, or bar-iron with hides and furs, beeswax, butter, wool, and balsam gum.

Farmers on Hazel Creek and similar mountain communities also produced a significant amount of corn liquor and fruit brandies as an important, and easily transportable, trade good. While the distilling practices and skills of Hazel Creekers would later cause a good deal of controversy and conflict, prior to the Civil War turning your surplus corn, peaches, or apples into liquor was a perfectly legal and perfectly respectable enterprise—the Baptists had yet to embrace teetotaling. Most families owned a still and possessed the skill to make palatable, if not prized, doubled-and-twisted liquor which found a ready market with local merchants. Of course most folks also kept some liquor on-hand for personal consumption and as the active ingredient in most folk cures. Duane Oliver noted that one of the first things Moses Proctor did on his farm was to plant a peach orchard. He used his skills as a distiller to make "brandy from these, useful for drinking, barter and as an addition to home-made herbal medicines."

While life on Hazel Creek before the Civil War was far from idyllic, the Proctors, Cables, Welches, and Bradshaws found a solid subsistence from the land and

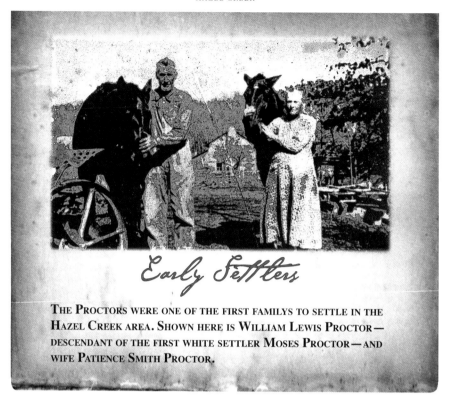

Early Settlers

**THE PROCTORS WERE ONE OF THE FIRST FAMILYS TO SETTLE IN THE
HAZEL CREEK AREA. SHOWN HERE IS WILLIAM LEWIS PROCTOR—
DESCENDANT OF THE FIRST WHITE SETTLER MOSES PROCTOR—AND
WIFE PATIENCE SMITH PROCTOR.**

ways to supplement that basic subsistence through market participation.

The sound and fury of Civil War battle never came to Hazel Creek itself, but the area's isolation did not protect the people or the land from its effects. Given their connections to deeply Unionist Cades Cove and the fact that none of the residents held slaves, it is somewhat surprising that all of the families living on the creek sided with the Confederacy. All seven able-bodied young men—Mansfield, Moses, Jr., James, and William Proctor, Josiah Bradshaw, and two Joseph Welches—served in the 9th Regiment of the Army of Northern Virginia. The war took a heavy toll on the young soldiers; Mansfield Proctor died in battle in Virginia, Moses Proctor, Jr. died of typhoid, James Proctor was captured and held as a P. O. W. in Illinois, and Joseph Welch contracted smallpox, almost died, and lost an eye. The survivors returned to Hazel Creek after the war, battered physically and mentally.

Life was no picnic for the older men, women, and children left behind to tend the farms and subsist under challenging circumstances. While fears for the safety of sons, husbands, and brothers in harm's way somewhere far away weighed on them, more immediate fears took their toll as well. Both Confederate and Unionist raiders regularly passed through the area leaving Hazel Creek residents in fear for their own personal safety and their sparse supplies and belongings.

Losing the most able-bodied men and the effective shut down of market relations and trade routes for the duration of the war made subsistence particularly challenging for those left behind. Many of the women of the area probably felt like another woman in western North Carolina who wrote to a Raleigh newspaper editor decrying the impact of losing all the young men on her family and mountain community: "Will you be so kind, Mr. Editor, as to inform Jeff Davis and his Destructives, that after they take the next draw of men [draft] from this mountain region, if they please, as an act of *great* and *special* mercy be so gracious as to call out a *few*, just a few of their exempted pets... to knock the women and children of the mountains in the head, to put them out of their misery."

In the years after the war, the folks on Hazel Creek began to pick up the pieces and continue on with life. Change did not come quickly to the area, but change was on the horizon. While there was no land rush, more families moved into the area in the 1870s and '80s, pushing settlement up Hazel Creek and up its tributaries of Sugar Fork, Bone Valley Creek, and Walkers Creek. One of the more significant families to move in at this time was the Calhoun family who moved over the ridge from Wayside around 1886. Granville Calhoun—who was ten at the time and who lived to the age of 104 and became one of the most important sources of information on life in Hazel Creek from the 1880s up to the 1940s—recalled the family's move to the upper reaches of Hazel Creek: "No, no road! My father sort of chopped out a road, and we were the first people ever to take a wagon up in there. He went there, and had this nice little piece of land, it was nice little level land, and he took a fancy to it for some reason... he could raise his corn and taters and cabbage. Anything you could raise..."

As more families moved into the area, the trappings of community began to develop up and down the creek. In 1875, Catherine and Joseph Welch built the Proctor school on land inherited from Moses Proctor. While most of the children of the earliest settlers learned to read and write in the home—and most were apparently literate—so-called "subscription schools" charging $1 per month for a three to four month school year cropped up in the 1870s on Bone Valley, Walkers Creek, and Cable Branch.

On one or two Sundays a month, these tiny schools doubled as church houses with the folks on Hazel Creek seeming to be as unanimously Baptist as they were unanimously Confederate. The preachers themselves were community members who had no special theological training, but who felt a "calling" confirmed by the community. Duane Oliver records Benson Cook, Marion Medlin, and Fonz Marcus as the early pastors in the area. "Well-known revival minister" Joshua Calhoun moved to Bone Valley in 1884 and became noted throughout the region for his preaching, "especially against bootlegging and whiskey."

Church, and the Baptist faith, particularly the Primitive Baptist strain, were important community binders on Hazel Creek. Folks would walk for miles to attend church services or annual revival meetings. As Seymour Calhoun argued, "...you take the churches on one... say up on Hazel Creek, up around Bone Valley... Practically everybody on that creek, and maybe Eagle Creek, any of them within 4 or 5 miles—they didn't consider that more than an after supper walk—And anywhere there was meetings, like churches or any kind of public gathering, everybody in the neighborhood went, back and forth." As Horace Kephart observed, "Everybody goes. If one judged from attendance he would rate our highlanders as the most religious people in America."

Kephart described the scene at a typical service which often lasted as long as three hours. "The congregation ranges itself, men on one side, women on the other, on rude benches that sometimes have no backs." Services began with a capella singing using the old shaped-note system. As Duane Oliver observed: "A few people had hymnals, but practically everyone knew the hymns anyway, taking their cues from the minister or someone in the congregation with a strong voice and a good sense of pitch." After the singing, preachers held forth from the pulpit, with sermons heavy on the importance of repentance, redemption, and personal salvation delivered in an energetic and emotional tone. Preachers often lapsed into what some observers have termed, the "holy tone." As Kephart described it, "When he warms up, he throws in a gasping ah or uh at short intervals…" Services were not at all what modern church-goers generally experience, with a lively call and response between preacher and congregation, crying babies, and people—primarily men and boys—walking in and out of the church.

Church was both a sacred event and a social event for people with little social contact outside of the family. Indeed, the churchyard scene was as lively as the church itself as Kephart describes men and boys congregating "on the outside to whittle, gossip, drive bargains, and debate among themselves some point of dogma that is too good to keep still about." Oliver noted that church was also an important place for courting a spouse. "With such a comparatively few people living in the area, finding a suitable spouse who was not one's cousin was no easy task, and church gatherings were a fine place to make acquaintances."

When the summer approached, baptisms, revival meetings, and other special church events further bound the community together. As the weather warmed congregations gathered at designated pools in Hazel Creek or its tributaries to baptize those who had come forward at an altar call earlier in the year to "publicly profess their faith in Jesus" and "join the church." Dinners on the grounds often accompanied baptisms and made them day-long events. Special foot-washing and communion services and all-day singings also attracted big crowds to Hazel Creek churches.

In late summer, when the "crops were laid by"—meaning the fields had grown up to the point where they needed little weeding or tending—the community held revival or camp meetings. Usually, visiting evangelists came in for one week meetings with services often held twice a day, at 11:00 a.m. and then again in the evening. The Reverend George Britt recalled the religious intensity of these eagerly

The Bradshaws

THE BRADSHAW FAMILY WAS ONE OF THE "FIRST FAMILIES" OF
HAZEL CREEK. THEY LEFT THEIR DISTINCTIVE IMPRINT ON THE
LAND FOR OVER **90** YEARS.

anticipated events: "The preachers would climb the mountain across Hazel Creek, opposite the [Bone Valley] church, and pray each day loud enough to be heard great distances… As I look back today to those blessed days, those echoes vibrating from hill to hill, seem so similar to the Old Testament Prophets proclaiming 'Thus saith the Lord.'"

Nearly everyone within reasonable walking distance came. Reverend Britt recalled an era when the lines of separation between church and state were not so brightly drawn: "The children at Sugar Fork School would line up, two by two, and march over the hill to the eleven o'clock service during the revival."

Horace Kephart also recorded the importance of revivals to the Hazel Creek community but focused more on their social aspects rather than their religious impact. He especially noted the significance of the camp meeting for the more socially isolated in the community, particularly women and young people:

> It is a jubilee-week to the work-worn and home-chained women, their
> only diversion from a year of unspeakably monotonous toil. As for the young
> folks, it is their theater, their circus, their country fair. (I say this with no
> disrespect: 'big-meetin' time is a gala week, if there be any such thing at all

in the mountains—its attractiveness is full as much secular as spiritual to the great body of people.)"

Small community stores cropped up at the same time as school houses and churches and further bound the community together. Jimmy Bradshaw opened the first store at Proctor in the late 1870s. Marion Medlin opened a store near the head of Bone Valley in 1880. According to Duane Oliver, the storekeepers, or contracted teamsters, generally used the Parsons Turnpike to haul out trade goods and haul in wagon loads of supplies. The trip usually took at least a week. When the railroad arrived at Bushnell just down the Little Tennessee River, the trip became much shorter and easier. Storekeepers conducted business primarily on the barter system as customers traded skins and hides, eggs, butter, corn, and medicinal herbs for cloth, gunpowder, lead, and the few other necessities they did not make themselves. As Granville Calhoun told newspaper columnist John Parris: "Hard money was hard to come by in those days. Trade was carried on mostly by barter. Marion Medlin would sell the folks whatever they wanted for herbs, like ginseng. He would trade them calico and powder for ginseng and penny royal."

These early stores were very small and generally not much to look at. Duane Oliver described them as "one-room log structures either attached to or very close to the owner's cabins." Granville Calhoun shared that these stores were even less impressive on the inside: "Medlin's store wasn't much. The stock was pretty poor. He carried some calico and some powder and lead. A feller didn't have a store unless he carried powder and lead." Medlin was a typical rural store owner, and as such, a jack-of-all-trades. He simultaneously served as Justice of the Peace, a Baptist preacher, and, in Oliver's words, "a dispenser of medical nostrums."

Medlin also became the second postmaster on Hazel Creek when his store became the Medlin post office in 1887. The first came along in 1886 when Bradshaw's store was dubbed the Proctor post office. Mail delivery was a challenging proposition on Hazel Creek in the early days of the service. According to Horace Kephart, in the earliest stages young men carried the mail to Medlin on foot from the railhead at Bushnell, a 32-mile round trip. The ones who "toted the sacks on their own wethers' got 48 cents a day." Later, a contractor serving four other area communities employed riders to deliver and pick up the mail. As Kephart recalled, the contractor "had to furnish two horses, pay the rider, and squeeze his own profit, out of $499 a year."

While mail service was understandably slow, it did connect Hazel Creek to the outside world on a regular basis. Granville Calhoun recalled that his father subscribed to the *New York World*. As a result, he became a sort of community newscaster. "Everybody could find out what was going on. Get out on a Sunday and gather a whole crowd up, and they'd talk and he'd read it to them."

The stores/post offices of Hazel Creek also served as community gathering spots, particularly for men. They would come by in the evenings, share a smoke or a chew, re-hash any community, national, or international news that came up, and swap some lies. Seymour Calhoun recalled the occasional political gathering held outside stores during campaign season: "Oh, ever once in a while they'd have a little political gathering along about politicking time. Have a few fights, sort of entertain the public."

Another sign of community progress and expansion came with the construction of three overshot grist mills in the late 19th century. Much more efficient than the traditional tub mills, folks in the area could now haul their corn, wheat, and rye to these mills where the millers ground the grain in exchange for a portion of the meal. Josiah Bradshaw built the first near Proctor, while John Walker built one on the upper reaches of Hazel Creek, and the last was built on Cable Branch.

As the community aged, cemeteries also became key community touchstones. Moses Proctor, who died in 1864, was the first white person buried in Hazel Creek. He asked to be buried on a hill on his property which became the Proctor Cemetery, the largest in the community. According to Duane Oliver, "the law required that every householder had to provide a place on his land for the burial of his family." In Hazel Creek, where the churches never created their own cemeteries and there were no community cemeteries, at least nine family cemeteries were scattered through the watershed.

One new fact of life that divided the Hazel Creek community after the Civil War was the changing legal and moral status of alcohol and alcohol production. In 1862, Congress passed a revenue act which, up to the present day, made the production of untaxed alcohol a federal offense. Farmers who made liquor as part of their subsistence and market activities now became outlaws. While the national media called them "moonshiners," folks in the Smokies preferred the term "blockaders"— as in one who runs a blockade. Hazel Creek farmers had to make the decision, under challenging economic conditions, of whether they would abide by the federal law or continue with this traditional method of producing an important barter commodity and securing hard-to-come-by cash as outlaws.

Many folks in the area did not have difficulty in defying a distant and, since this was a staunchly Confederate community, even hostile federal government. In the words of authors Wilbur Ziegler and Ben Grosscup who visited and hunted in the Hazel Creek area in the early 1880s: "Now, the blockader, like the majority of drinking men, is a good-natured fellow, who, while he deems himself a citizen of the United States, confounds natural with civil liberty, and believes he has the right to manufacture, drink and sell whiskey in whatever manner he pleases so long as he does not interfere with the private rights of his neighbors."

A factor further complicating community attitudes toward alcohol and alcohol production was the rise of the temperance/prohibition movement in the late 19th century, particularly among Baptists. Preachers like Joshua Calhoun regularly railed against the evils of liquor from Hazel Creek pulpits. Indeed, by the early years of

The Cables

PEARL AND CARA WILLIAMS CABLE CA. 1920S ON THEIR WEDDING DAY ON HAZEL CREEK. LIKE THE PROCTORS THE CABLES MOVED ACROSS THE MOUNTAINS FROM CADES COVE AND LENT THEIR NAMES TO SEVERAL PLACES IN THE WATERSHED.

the 20th century, many Baptist churches had incorporated language condemning the "sale and use of intoxicating drinks as a beverage" into church covenants.

The assumption that many make, however, that one either chose the church or the liquor is an erroneous one. Particularly in rural Baptist churches, like those in Hazel Creek, the relationship was much more complex. As Durwood Dunn noted in his classic work on Cades Cove, "there existed from the Civil War onward an uneasy tension between those who drank [and made] moonshine and those who violently disapproved." Pastors and active parishioners understood both human frailty and the need, particularly at times of economic emergency, for farmers to supplement their income by making a run or two of liquor. As Dunn observed, this led to "their skillful application of a rule of social utility," whereby, "If a… farmer drank only moderately and if his main source of income was not from moonshining, his weakness was grudgingly tolerated." Indeed, even the most teetotaling pastor understood that tithes and offerings that built church buildings and helped pay them a meager salary often came from the proceeds from manufacturing and selling illegal liquor.

We will never truly know how many Hazel Creek farmers made illegal liquor as such people do not, as a rule, keep business records and community opprobrium has kept stories of family moonshine making in the shadows. According to Horace Kephart, who arrived on Hazel Creek in 1904, a very high percentage of men on Hazel Creek had experience in the business. "Now, when four men are picked up at random in our township [for a posse], it is safe to assume that at least three have been moonshiners themselves…" Duane Oliver, the most comprehensive chronicler of life on Hazel Creek, on the other hand contends that Kephart exaggerated the number of moonshiners to fit popular stereotypes of mountain people and for dramatic effect:

> It is a definite mistake to think of most mountain men as moonshiners as depicted in popular novels and movies set in the Smokies. A few did make illicit whiskey .. but they were decidedly in the minority. One of the faults with Horace Kephart's book *Our Southern Highlanders*, researched and written partly on Hazel Creek, is that he too much romanticized moonshining and bootlegging. They did exist on Hazel Creek when he was there and he, being an outsider, found them fascinating and overemphasized them in his book.

Zeigler and Grosscup observed in the 1880s: "Blockading, or 'moonshining' as it is sometimes called,… is not as prevalent in the mountains as is generally supposed; and besides, it is growing less with every year."

The truth, as usual, probably lies somewhere in between the observations of Kephart and Oliver. Most Hazel Creek farmers had the knowledge, skills, and access to the equipment and materials necessary to make blockade whiskey. Especially when young men just started out on their own, they also possessed an abiding need for some cash money for a grubstake or to tide them over an economic rough patch. These young men were generally seasonal moonshiners, not career moon-shiners. As they aged, and became more tied to family, church, and community and found some modicum of economic security, they became less likely to risk both their freedom and their reputation. As they matured they eschewed the moonshine business and they, and family, pretended that they were never involved.

Some folks in the area, however, did take the blockade liquor business on as their chosen career, despite community censure. Aquilla "Quill" Rose, from just across Pinnacle Ridge on Eagle Creek, became somewhat of a nationally known celebrity moonshiner. Rose first claimed notoriety as a combination hunting guide and moonshiner in Zeigler and Grosscup's 1883 book, *Heart of the Alleghenies*. The authors characterized Quill and his brother Jake in terms that became increasingly familiar to the American public as not only common to moonshiners, but common to residents of rural southern Appalachian communities in general. Ziegler and Grosscup asserted that Quill and Jake were "good-natured" and hospitable, but "when aroused" became men "of desperate character." They continued with their assessment emphasizing the brothers' cussedly independent and violent character:

> They have been blockaders. Living outside of school districts, and
> seemingly all State protection, they refuse to pay any taxes; having only a
> trailway to their door, they pay no attention to notices for working the county
> roads. Thus recognizing no authority, they live in a pure state of natural
> liberty, depending for its continance upon their own strength and daring, the
> fears of county officers, the seclusion of their home, and their proximity to
> the Tennessee line. Only one and a half mile of mountain ascent is required
> to place them beyond the pursuit of State authorities. One of them killed his
> man, in Swain County, and to this day he has escaped trial. They are men
> of fine features and physique. Both wear full, dark beards; long, black hair;
> slouch hats; blue hunting shirts, uncovered by coats or vests, and belted with
> a strop holding their pantaloons in place. High boots with exposed tops, cover
> their feet and lower limbs. They are tall and broad-shouldered.

Quill became even more famous when he cropped up in several magazine articles written by Kephart and in *Our Southern Highlanders*. Kephart quotes an oft-told story about Quill and his views on the benefits of aging liquor:

> "A slick-faced dude from Knoxville told me once that all good red-liquor
> was aged, and that if I'd age my blockade it would bring a fancy price. Well sir,
> I tried it; I kept some for three months—and by godlings, *it ain't so*." Duane
> Oliver's grandmother Sadie Farley told him that Rose once had a still on the
> state line in the Smokies "so that he could cross over in the adjoining state if

Joseph Washington Welch

JOSEPH WELCH OF FORNEY CREEK MARRIED CATHERINE PROCTOR AND THEY BECAME THE SECOND HOMEOWNERS ON HAZEL CREEK. WELCH FILED FOR TWO 50-ACRE LAND GRANTS FROM THE STATE IN 1849. JOSIAH AND SARAH BRADSHAW SOON JOINED THEM. THE PROCTORS, CABLES, WELCHES, AND BRADSHAWS AND THEIR DESCENDANTS FORMED THE BACKBONE OF THE HAZEL CREEK COMMUNITY FOR THE NEXT 90-PLUS YEARS.

raided." Quill often crossed the ridge and came into Hazel Creek for business and pleasure. Oliver's grandmother also told him that Rose once commented to her that his "'scorpion juice' would be good for what ailed her."

While Quill and Jake lived in the Eagle Creek watershed, they became commonly attached in the popular mind to the Hazel Creek community. As a result of these stereotypical characterizations by Ziegler and Grosscup, Kephart, and later authors, Hazel Creek and its residents became, unfortunately and inaccurately, portrayed as exemplars of the "strange and peculiar" people who inhabited the isolated mountain coves and hollows of southern Appalachia.

Despite these stereotypes, by the late 1880s, Hazel Creek had taken on the

Aquilla "Quill" Rose

AQUILLA ROSE WAS A LEGENDARY MOUNTAINEER, BEAR
HUNTER, BLOCKADER, AND COLORFUL CHARACTER WHO
LIVED ON EAGLE CREEK. HE RECOGNIZED NO AUTHORITY
SAVE HIS OWN AND BUILT HIS CABIN WITHIN ONE AND A HALF
MILES OF THE STATE LINE, ENSURING HIS ABILITY TO EVADE
REVENUERS, LOCAL LAW MEN, AND GRUDGE HOLDERS.

character of a fairly typical rural mountain community with two post offices, three stores, and four schools that doubled as Baptist churches. While transportation in and out of the community was challenging for sure and the pace of life moved more slowly than in areas with more efficient lines of transportation and communication, folks in Hazel Creek were aware of the rapidly changing world outside the mountains and were tied to that world, albeit in a limited fashion, by market relationships.

At the same time, however, the look of the land in and around Hazel Creek had not changed a lot since Moses Proctor came over the mountain from Cades Cove into Possum Hollow. Indeed, the human environmental footprint had not changed much, except for the impact of domestic animals, from the days when the Cherokee hunted, gathered, and planted in the watershed. From the state line ridge of the Smokies looking down on Hazel Creek, the land looked much as it had for millennia. Ziegler and Grosscup recorded their impressions of that view from Clingmans Dome in *Heart of the Alleghenies*:

> On all sides stretch wild, black forests, funereal in their aspect, wakened only by the cry of the raven, or the tinkle of the bell of some animal lost in their labyrinths. The great wilderness of the deciduous trees lie below, mantling ridges and hollows. In vain the eye endeavors to mark their limit; it is blanketed by the misty purple into which the green resolves itself. Here, for the bear, deer, wolf, and panther appears the natural home. Nowhere is there a more perfect roaming ground for those animals; but the hound, rifle, and trap, brought into active use by the Indians and mountaineers, have greatly thinned out the game; still, no better hunting is to be found east of the Mississippi.

But dramatic change for Hazel Creek was on the horizon, heralded by the piercing sound of a train whistle as it pulled into the station at Bushnell. In a very short time, the wolf and panther would be gone from the area, probably forever. And that "great wilderness of the deciduous trees" would begin to fall in great swaths to the woodhick's axe and crosscut saw. The coming of the industrial revolution changed not only the landscape, but the people of Hazel Creek as well.

The coming of the railroad to Bushnell in 1889 began a period of rapid change in the Hazel Creek watershed as industrial timber and mining operations moved into the area. For the next fifty-plus years, the communities of Hazel Creek would witness and experience firsthand the best and the worst of the boom-and-bust cycles that characterized the early period of industrial revolution in the United States. Indeed, the community experienced a kind of cultural whiplash with the comings and goings of railroads, industrial operations, thousands of new residents, improved communication facilities, stores, movie theaters, schools, roads, and, later, the federal government.

The first industrial boom on Hazel Creek began in 1892 with the arrival of the Taylor & Crate Lumber Company from New York. The Hazel Creek watershed had long been known for some of the richest hardwood timber lands in North America. The area teemed with huge chestnuts, tulip poplars, ash, cucumber, basswood, oak, and maple. Despite the richness of the forests, the challenges of transporting timber to mill kept land prices and the prices of timber rights (where the owner still held title to the land but gave up the rights to cut timber), extremely low.

In order to facilitate the purchase of land or timber rights and get their operations going, Taylor & Crate hired experienced logger, agent, and timber cruiser Jack Coburn. Coburn moved to the area in 1888 from Michigan after much of that state's old-growth forest was cut over and worked for the Heyser Lumber Company at their Fairfax logging camp. In the early 1890s, Coburn began buying up

Granville Calhoun

GRANVILLE CALHOUN, FOURTH FROM RIGHT, MOVED TO HAZEL CREEK
WHEN HE WAS TEN YEARS OLD AND LIVED TO BE 104. HE PLAYED A PIVOTAL
ROLE IN ALMOST EVERY HISTORICAL EVENT IN HAZEL CREEK FROM THE
1880S TO THE 1940S AND BECAME ONE OF THE BEST SOURCES FOR THE
HISTORY OF THE AREA.

timber rights near the banks of Hazel Creek and its major tributaries. According to
historian Jim Casada, Coburn became "quite possibly the wealthiest man in Swain
County" as a "land broker, timber dealer, real estate agent, investor, and entrepreneur…" He built a home at the confluence of Bone Valley Creek and Hazel Creek
and maintained a separate residence in Bryson City.

With no railroad access in the area, Taylor & Crate planned to use a logging
method common to the big woods of the upper Midwest, cutting near the banks of
streams, skidding the logs to the stream edge, then floating the logs downstream to a
larger river or lake — in this case the Little Tennessee River — chaining logs together in rafts, and then using a steamboat to pull the rafts downstream to mills. The
timber from Hazel Creek logged by Taylor & Crate crews made an approximately
150-mile trip downstream to mills near Chattanooga, Tennessee.

In order to make sure the streams had enough water and force to drive the
huge logs down the creeks and into the Little Tennessee, Taylor & Crate built three
"splash dams" in the Hazel Creek watershed to back up the waters. The company
hired Granville Calhoun, a man who played a pivotal role in almost every important
historical juncture in the watershed from the 1880s to the 1940s, to help build the

dams. Years later, he recalled constructing one hemlock-log dam 250 feet wide, 18 feet high, with an opening 16 feet wide. Timber company workers built dams near the Crate Hall place on Bone Valley Creek, just below the mouth of Walkers Creek on the upper reaches of Hazel Creek, and just below a big bend on Hazel Creek at Proctor. Workers also bored holes in large rocks in the creeks and dynamited them and cleared the streams of timber and brush not commercially valuable in order to ease the flow of timber.

Once workers made these preparations, loggers—generally known as woodhicks in the Smokies—took to the forest with their crosscut saws and axes and began selectively cutting trees along the streams, focusing only on the most valuable, and best floating, timber; poplar, ash, and cucumber. Granville Calhoun asserted Taylor & Crate was also highly selective as to the quality of the timber as well. "They wouldn't put an ax or saw to a tree if it had two knots in it." After felling the trees, the woodhicks trimmed the branches and sawed the trees into manageable lengths. They then either let gravity do the work and "ballhooted" the logs down steep banks to the stream or used oxen to skid them into the water.

Once the loggers had enough timber in the streams, one of the most awesomely destructive sights ever devised by humans ensued. Coordinating their efforts so that the "head" of water hit the confluence of Bone Valley and Hazel Creeks at the same time, workers opened the floodgates and released a torrent of water into the streams. Granville Calhoun eloquently described the subsequent sights and sounds to reporter John Parris:

"When that gate was raised, the water would go out with a roar. Now I tell you, it was something to see. It would flood the creek all the way… When that happened the logs went rolling and tumbling and the water roaring, you could hear it for a mile. It was like a storm, the logs bumping one another and hitting the rocks."

As water and logs rushed downstream, the woodhicks, wearing caulked—or as they called them in the Smokies, "corked"—boots with spikes in the soles and bearing long, iron-tipped pike poles, took to the creeks to free log jams and keep things flowing. As one would expect, this was incredibly dangerous work requiring balance and skill to keep from falling and being crushed by the logs or drowned in the rushing waters. In its short five or six years of operation, three Taylor & Crate woodhicks—Marion Myers, Bud Welch, and Will Bradshaw—lost their lives with countless unnamed others hurt or maimed.

Despite the dangers of the work, many, if not most, of the young men living on Hazel Creek spent at least some time working the woods for Taylor & Crate. As Duane Oliver observed: "A considerable number of the able-bodied men of Hazel Creek and from neighboring areas worked for the lumber company in cutting timber, handling ox teams, building the dams and seeing that the logs got down the creek to the river and beyond." The details of this period in Hazel Creek's history are relatively sketchy, but the work was probably seasonal, and while it did provide cash wages, it served primarily as a supplement to income from traditional agricultural activities.

Although few Hazel Creek residents commented on it at the time, this process of driving logs downstream with a torrent of water was highly destructive of the environment. The flooding waters and huge trees rushing downstream gouged the stream banks and caused erosion. The flood of water and trees also had a devastating impact on fish, otters, and other aquatic life. Granville Calhoun lamented this fact but also reaped a bounty from the floods: "The splash dams practically destroyed all the native trout. When they cut loose they would kill fish and wash them over the banks of the creek, leaving them in little puddles. Folks used to go and dip them up by the buckets full. Always after I let the dams loose, and the flood had subsided, I would go down the creek and get me a mess of fish."

The Taylor & Crate timber operation lasted only five or six years and the woodhicks floated the last trees downstream in 1898. By that time, the company had cut most of the easily accessible and floatable timber. As Granville Calhoun observed, they cut "only what was easy to get to and didn't require moving any great distance." As testimony to the rich timber resources in the watershed, even with the limitations of its operations, according to Calhoun, Taylor & Crate cut more than a million board-feet of timber in the 1890s.

Despite its short tenure in the Hazel Creek watershed, the Taylor & Crate era transformed the area in a number of important ways. It ushered in a new era of cash wages and industrial work that changed the lives of almost everyone in the area and, for better and worse, caught them up in the currents of the modern world almost as tumultuous as the head of water created by the splash dams. It also brought the first major visible changes to the landscape since the first humans arrived as banks were cleared of timber and the streambeds gouged by the floods. It brought less visible but important changes to the ecology of the area by eliminating forest cover for wildlife, killing aquatic life, and clouding the once clear-flowing streams with sediment.

The second era of industrial development in the Hazel Creek watershed followed on the heels of Taylor & Crate's timber operations and was the result of a chance discovery by Jacob Fonslow "Fonzie" Hall around 1883. While visiting his brother Crate, Fonzie went out prospecting for mica on Little Fork Ridge when he came across what he thought was gold. Fonzie soon found out, however, that he had discovered copper. Given the deposit's remote location and the low price of copper at the time, the find was not worth developing. However, word soon spread of Fonzie's find including to the owner of the land, local land speculator and politician Ep Everett, who began looking for a buyer who had the capital and knowledge to develop a mine.

Fonzie Hall was probably not the first person to find copper in the Hazel Creek area. The Cherokee most likely knew about it and according to Duane Oliver, Robert McCampbell of Cades Cove came over to do some prospecting in the 1830s.

Loggers

Loggers—known as "woodhicks" in the Smokies—cleared the old-growth hardwood forests of Hazel Creek using crosscut saws ("misery whips") and axes.

Others, including Dr. Calvin Post, poked around the area and found evidence of copper around 1850 and Stephen Mundy bought up considerable land in the area with the intention of developing its copper and timber resources. The Hazel Creek, and nearby Eagle Creek, ore veins are an extension of the rich deposits located to the west in the Ducktown/Copperhill area of East Tennessee which developers opened for mining in 1850. While the Hazel Creek and Eagle Creek ores were richer in copper than those in East Tennessee, the remoteness of the area and the relatively small overall size of the deposits kept mine developers away, at least until Fonzie Hall and a railhead at Bushnell, came along.

Ep Everett finally found his buyer in the late 1890s in mining entrepreneur W. S. Adams of Boston who visited the site, had the ore assayed, and seeing the site's richness and with a railhead only 25 miles or so away from the site at Bushnell, purchased 200 acres for $662.50. Developing the site required a good deal of capital investment from Adams who not only had to hire men to work the mine, but had to build workshops, a gunpowder house, housing for workers, and a cookhouse. He also had to improve the local roads to facilitate transport of the ore to Bushnell and even constructed a new road alongside Hazel Creek so the ore could be transported to the Little Tennessee River then hauled upstream along a pre-existing road to

Adams-Westfeldt Mine

COPPER MINING PROVIDED AN ADDITIONAL INTRODUCTION TO THE MODERN INDUSTRIAL WORLD AND WAGE LABOR FOR HAZEL CREEK RESIDENTS. HOWEVER, THE 26-YEAR-LONG LAWSUIT BETWEEN ADAMS AND WESTFELDT KEPT THE MINE CLOSED FOR MUCH OF THE 20TH CENTURY.

Bushnell. Trains then hauled the ore to smelters in the Ducktown/Coppertown area.

One of the first men hired by Adams was, of course, Granville Calhoun. As Calhoun recalled, Adams hired inexperienced locals to do the mining by hand: "We went to work in there with just pick and shovels… I took charge of it from the very first pick they ever struck. And I didn't know, I'd never been inside of a tunnel or anything." Adams soon expanded his operations, brought in additional laborers from outside, and purchased steam-powered equipment to move miners and tools into the mines and bring out the ore. Miners eventually dug thirteen, five-feet-wide by seven feet tall shafts to access the ore. The Adams mine, at its peak of operation, reportedly employed more than a hundred men working in shifts.

One of Adams' plans for the mine fortunately never came to fruition. In order to lessen the amount of material he had to haul to the smelters, Adams planned to follow a pattern set at the Copperhill/Ducktown copper mines in nearby East Tennessee and build an open-heap roaster to burn off some of the impurities from the ore. This process of heaping ore, covering it with wood, and then continuing to build up alternating layers, then setting it on fire creates an environmentally destructive double-whammy. First, the process consumes huge amounts of wood, leading to the clear-cutting of local forests. Secondly, the process creates a toxic plume of sulfuric acid. As historian Lance Holland observed, "The gaseous acid is heavier than air, sinks to the ground, and kills all vegetation it contacts." Anyone who ever saw the Copperhill/Ducktown area in the 20th century will know that the result of this process was a veritable desert. Fortunately, a land dispute and lawsuit that dragged on for 26 years and outlived both litigants spared Hazel Creek this fate as mining came to an abrupt halt in 1901.

Land disputes were common in the Hazel Creek area, and in the southern Appalachian region in general. Marking land boundaries in the 19th century was a pretty inexact science, particularly when surveyors used vague markers such as "a birch on the waters of Hazel Creek." As Horace Kephart observed, "Titles were confused, owing to careless surveys, or guesswork, in the past. Many boundaries overlapped, and there were bits of no-man's land here and there, covered by no deed and subject to entry by anyone who discovered them." Since many of the speculators who held much of the land in the Hazel Creek watershed lived far away and had never actually visited the land they owned, issues of clear title did not usually arise until owners tried to sell their land or when someone discovered a valuable resource. Then it was up to the courts to sift through the records and make a determination as to who held proper title.

The dispute over the Adams mine arose when New Orleans land speculator George Westfeldt, who had bought 640 acres of Hazel Creek watershed land in 1869, evidently heard about the mine and began to develop a mine on his own nearby property. Westfeldt apparently started his mining operation not far from the Adams mine on a prong of the Sugar Fork around 1900. The remains of an Orr & Sembower steam-powered hoist, parts of it still at the site, testify to the investment Westfeldt made in the mine. The hoist lowered men and equipment down a 110-foot vertical shaft and hauled the ore out. It is not known how many horizontal shafts miners dug off of the vertical shaft or how much ore came out of the mine. Westfeldt became convinced that Adams had encroached on his land and filed suit to stop the mining and resolve the title. Both sides claimed the other side moved survey markers and/or falsified records. In 1901, the court granted Westfeldt an injunction until the courts settled the boundary issue and mining at both sites ceased. The lawsuit became increasingly acrimonious with neither Adams nor Westfeldt willing to give an inch. The case, and its many appeals, dragged on for 26 years, reportedly gainfully employed 11 lawyers, and helped fund area courts to the tune of $500,000. The court finally decided in Adams' favor in 1927, but in a manner befitting an Aesop's Fable, long after both men had died.

The early logging and mining era changed forever the lives of the people living in the Hazel Creek region. Most of the residents for the first time became at least partially dependent on cash wages, a factor that made the times of bust even tougher. Local store owners benefited from the new business as they sold more factory-made cloth and clothing and even foodstuffs ordinarily grown on the farm.

Before his tragic death, Will Bradshaw kept an account book of his expenditures at the Medlin store. His 1896 purchases included a pair of socks (25 cents), a pair of pants ($1.00), two shirts (50 cents and 30 cents), 40 cents worth of tobacco, one-half bushel of corn (25 cents), and three yards of cloth for 25 cents.

The new era also brought many newcomers to Hazel Creek. Although it is hard to pinpoint exactly where they lived, based on the 1900 census it appears that about 27 families lived in the Hazel Creek watershed. By Horace Kephart's count in 1905, enumerated on a map he created, there were about 42 families living in the watershed by that point. Neither is an exact count and it is hard to know who was missed in the census or by Kephart, but it is obvious that the community was growing in the late 19th and early 20th centuries attracting Moores, Crisps, Walkers, Buchanans, Gunters, Cogdills, Copes, Brendles, Hamptons, Joneses, Myerses, Laneys, Wilsons, Davises, Flowerses, Hensleys, and Cooks to join the many branches of the early-arriving Proctor, Bradshaw, Cable, Welch, Calhoun, and Hall families.

Industry also brought some not so welcome changes to the community, as young men with cash money naturally got into mischief involving moonshine, cockfighting, fisticuffs, and firearms. While events such as cockfights happened relatively frequently, Granville Calhoun recalled one particularly notorious battle in the heyday of the Adams mine. A "regular chicken man" by the name of Lovin from Graham County conspired with the well-known liquor-making Rose clan to have a chicken fight on Hazel Creek. Lovin would provide the chickens and the Roses the liquor. As often happened, as those gathered consumed more and more liquor the event deteriorated into a fight. One of the Rose boys shot Jess Cable in the arm and knocked one of his friends out cold. Jess and his brother Jake went home, retrieved a .38 Winchester rifle and lay in wait for the Roses as they returned to Eagle Creek. Jess shot one of them in the liver and Jess and Jake both ended up in the Swain County jail. If nothing else, the new era gave local preachers plenty to preach against.

With the closing of the Adams and Westfeldt mines in 1901, the community experienced its first bust cycle until a new era of industrial logging, this time using railroads and heavy steam-powered equipment, arrived with the coming of the Ritter Lumber Company. Ironically, Horace Kephart made his detailed observations of life on Hazel Creek during this period of bust between industrial booms. Those observations formed the heart of his classic book *Our Southern Highlanders* and shaped the views of educated Americans on the people and culture of the southern Appalachian region for generations.

Kephart arrived on Hazel Creek in November 1904, moved into one of the abandoned miner's shacks at the Adams mine on Sugar Fork, and lived there a little over one year until January 1906. He described a Hazel Creek community of 42 households, about 200 people, living primarily in log dwellings, many of them not even on a road capable of traversing in a wagon. The closest "civilization" to his cabin was two miles away in Medlin which Kephart described as "two little stores built of rough planks and bearing no signs, a corn mill, and four dwellings." A log schoolhouse, "which, once or twice a month, served also as a church," was located a mile-and-a-half away from Medlin. Kephart estimated that two-thirds of the residents owned their homes and land with the other one-third either renting or squatting. Kephart asserted that these squatters, "were permitted to occupy ground for the sake of reporting trespass and putting out fires—or, maybe, to prevent them doing both."

Kephart reported that almost everyone in the community scratched out a hard-scrabble existence on marginal farm land using a "bull-tongue" plow. He described the land in the area, in the words of one resident, as "so poor hit wouldn't raise a cuss-fight." Another neighbor reportedly commented, "This is good strong land, or it wouldn't hold up all the rocks there is around hyur." Kephart also observed their herding practices of allowing hogs to free-range in the forest and pasturing cattle on mountain balds. To supplement their income, folks gathered ginseng, bloodroot, wild ginger, or galax. An inordinate number of Hazel Creek folks, according to Kephart, further supplemented their income by making moonshine and *Our Southern Highlanders* is replete with their escapades and adventures in evading the law and plying their illegal trade. The author reported no one living in the area mining, cutting the timber, or in any occupation other than farming or storekeeping and never acknowledged the previous existence of such occupations in the community despite the fact he reported living in a mining shack.

Kephart described the Hazel Creek area as a "Back of Beyond," isolated from the outside world and locked in the 18th, or even the 17th, century, a place where he "might realize the past in the present, seeing with my own eyes what life must have been to my pioneer ancestors of a century or two ago." Kephart especially emphasized the role of isolation in shaping the attitudes and character of the people of Hazel Creek:

> No one can understand the attitude of our highlanders toward the rest of the earth until he realizes their amazing isolation from all that lies beyond the blue, hazy skyline of their mountains. Conceive a shipload of emigrants cast away on some unknown island, far from the regular track of vessels, and left there for five or six generations, unaided and untroubled by the growth of civilization. Among the descendants of such a company we would expect to find customs and ideas unaltered from the time of their forefathers. And that is just what we do find today among our castaways in the sea of mountains. Time has lingered in Appalachia. The mountain folk still live in the eighteenth century. The progress of mankind from that to this is no heritage of theirs.

While Kephart gives a somewhat sympathetic portrait of the denizens of Hazel

Creek, he argued their isolation, lack of education, and reliance on primitive ways condemned them to poverty. Kephart noted that the people were "kind-hearted, loyal to their friends, quick to help anyone in distress." At the same time, their "Rip Van Winkle sleep" and the "law of nature that dooms an isolated and impoverished people to deterioration" put them in a pitiable situation, although they themselves would never admit that.

On closer examination, however, it appears that far from encountering a static people who had lived an unchanging existence, holed up in a holler for generations, marrying their cousins, locked in the 18th century, and "deteriorating," the Hazel Creek that Kephart encountered was a place already shaped by the modern world and the industrial revolution, but one in the midst of a bust period. According to Duane Oliver, Kephart was very selective in what he chose to write: "This book [*Our Southern Highlanders*] angered many Hazel Creek people for they felt he had painted a picture of all of them as being lazy, destitute and ignorant. He was not interested in the ordinary people of Hazel Creek but the more picturesque inhabitants such as bootleggers, moonshiners and bearhunters as well as those living in extreme poverty." In a 1978 interview with journalist Carson Brewer, Granville Calhoun criticized Kephart's assertion that some Hazel Creek residents "went all winter without shoes." Calhoun recalled that he did not know anyone in the area without at least one pair of shoes. "Some didn't wear them on mild winter days, but they owned them."

To be sure, Kephart did pick and choose the people in the community he wanted to write about and devoted an inordinate portion of the book to the more exotic aspects of life and culture on Hazel Creek, particularly its moonshiners. Oliver asserts that Kephart "too much romanticized moonshining and bootlegging. They did exist on Hazel Creek when he was there and he, being an outsider, found them fascinating and overemphasized them in his book." Kephart, as one who made his living as a writer would do, had his eye on what his readers would enjoy and find entertaining. In addition, given the time period when he was in Hazel Creek, he probably did encounter a good number of moonshiners. One must remember that moonshining was most often the poor man's source of emergency cash in times of economic downturn. The folks on Hazel Creek were definitely in the midst of such a time when Kephart arrived and it is likely that in a period of industrial bust a majority of the men in the community had some involvement in the illegal liquor business, the most reliable source of ready cash. At the same time, Oliver is correct in observing that in the long-term, particularly after new industry arrived, moonshiners became a minority.

In the years after its publication, others also criticized Kephart's depiction of life on Hazel Creek, most notably local judge Felix E. Alley in his 1941 book *Random Thoughts and Musings of a Mountaineer*. While asserting that he knew Kephart "intimately," Alley took him and fellow author Margaret Morley, whose popular 1913 book *The Carolina Mountains* contained many of the same stereotypical characterizations of mountain people as *Our Southern Highlanders*, to task. Alley contended that the very popularity of these books and their "wide circulation... has tended to confirm and extend the false impression created by other libelous writers, so that even today multitudes of people both within and outside North Carolina look upon our mountaineers as freaks and curiosities."

Another important factor to consider in evaluating Kephart's picture of Hazel Creek is that based on the census records and Kephart's own map most of the residents of the community had arrived relatively recently attracted by the logging and mining jobs available. As historian Stephen Taylor observed in his work *The New South's New Frontier*, the people of the upper Little Tennessee valley "far from stuck in time and space, moved about so frequently that their connections to a particular family dwelling or ancestral homeplace lasted no more than a generation. Furthermore, entire communities came and went as industry and employment did."

The poverty Kephart observed was a product of long-term rural economic decline common across the United States and the loss of cash-paying jobs when Crate & Hall ceased operations and the Adams and Westfeldt mines closed. Being relatively new to the community, many of these now unemployed loggers and miners faced the prospect of farming the most marginal land in the area, as early arrivers had already claimed the most arable land. Their other major alternative was to leave the community altogether and seek opportunity elsewhere. Kephart did record the fact that "A little colony of our Hazel Creek people took a notion to try the Georgia cotton mills," but most "returned as soon as they possibly could." Oliver noted that in the period between industrial booms recruiters from Gastonia, North Carolina cotton mills came into the watershed seeking laborers. Given the circumstances, they found a good many takers and as Oliver observed, "many men moved from the mountains to become spinners rather than farmers or loggers."

A significant number of the residents of Hazel Creek, however, stayed in the community, decided to ride out the bust times, and in the words of Stephen Taylor tried, as best they could, to "get by." This meant doing anything and everything to provide for their families. Most raised corn and hogs, planted gardens, herded a few cattle, gathered herbs, made some moonshine, provided labor for neighbors, hunted and fished, and bartered skills as blacksmiths or carpenters. Historian Crandall Shifflet has referred to this as creating a "patchwork quilt" existence, and like good quilters, they used everything they had at hand, plus their own ingenuity and creativity, to stitch together their lives.

Unfortunately, complexities and context were not what consumers of popular culture in the early 20th century sought and Kephart's portrayal of Hazel Creek and of southern Appalachian culture became deeply ingrained in the national consciousness, even among academics. Kephart's depictions of mountain life even made it to Hollywood, most notably Karl Brown's popular and acclaimed 1927 production "Stark Love," a movie replete with classic Appalachian stereotypes. Filmed in nearby Graham County in 1926, Brown, in the words of Kephart biographer George Ellison, "was an ardent admirer of *Our Southern Highlanders*." Brown even hired Kephart "as a consultant on locations and mountaineer etiquette."

By the time the Outing Publishing Company published *Our Southern Highlanders* in 1913, however, Hazel Creek residents were too caught up in the decidedly modern drama of transformative industrial boom to care much about their image in popular culture as isolated hillbillies locked in the 18th century. Indeed, even as folks scratched by during the bust years and as Kephart wandered the watershed taking his copious notes, buyers for the largest hardwood timber company in the United States combed the ridges and coves, graded the timber, poured over land records in the Swain County courthouse, and quietly bought up land or timber rights to one of the richest tracts of hardwood anywhere, an area Kephart called, "One of the finest primeval forests in the world." Indeed, Kephart got out well before the new boom hit, anticipating the major changes on the horizon.

Horace Kephart

HORACE KEPHART DESCRIBED THE HAZEL CREEK WATER-
SHED HE FIRST ENCOUNTERED IN 1904 AS THE "BACK OF
BEYOND." KEPHART'S EXPERIENCES IN THE AREA FORMED
THE BACKBONE OF HIS CLASSIC WORK *OUR SOUTHERN
HIGHLANDERS*.

CHAPTER THREE

Boom Times

*H*azel Creek's second industrial boom period had quiet beginnings when representatives of the W. M. Ritter Lumber Company of Columbus, Ohio arrived in the area around 1902 or 1903. As the largest lumber company in the United States, Ritter already had sizable operations in West Virginia, Kentucky, Virginia, and other parts of western North Carolina. The company specialized in hardwood and in Hazel Creek they encountered a rich forest of huge oaks, poplars, chestnuts, maples, beeches, and basswoods that would justify its sizable capital investment in land, timber rights, railroads, steam loaders and skidders, saw mills, planing mills, drying kilns, homes for a workforce numbering in the hundreds, and facilities and infrastructure for a town nearing 1,000 inhabitants. Company representatives spent the early years of the 1900s securing rights to cut the timber and purchasing land for railroad right-of-ways and for town and mill sites. Land in Hazel Creek was cheap and timber rights were still cheaper given the area's distance from railroads or major roads. Duane Oliver reported that John Farley sold timber rights to 33 acres to Ritter for $300, and was probably ecstatic to get the offer.

Given the lean bust years after the closing of the mines, most folks on Hazel Creek were thrilled with the new possibilities for cash-paying jobs. As Granville Calhoun recalled, "Everybody wanted them to come in." His son Seymour agreed, "That meant a job for us, that meant some work to do."

However, not all community members welcomed Ritter, and its new jobs, to the community with open arms. Jimmy Bradshaw and Joseph Welch resisted selling

Ritter Train Depot

THE RITTER TRAIN DEPOT WAS AN IMPORTANT MARKER OF THE ARRIVAL, IN FULL FORCE, OF THE MODERN INDUSTRIAL WORLD ON HAZEL CREEK.

land they held in common in the Proctor area Ritter believed essential to their plans. The timber company took the men to court in 1907 and the court forced the men to sell in a condemnation suit. Bradshaw probably resisted because he knew his small store would be unable to compete with the coming company commissary. Horace Kephart was also not a fan of the changes he saw coming. On a bear hunt with Granville Calhoun and other Hazel Creekers he "heard the snort of a locomotive" on the Little River Railroad on the Tennessee side of the Smokies divide. "With a steam-loader and three camps of a hundred men each it was despoiling the Tennessee forest. Slowly, but inexorably, a leviathan was crawling into the wilderness and was soon to consume it." Few others in the community, however, thought much about the environmental or social consequences of such "progress."

Ritter's next order of business in the first decade of the 20th century was to construct a railroad into the area to access its timber. Given the potential business it would receive once Ritter started its operations, the Southern Railroad extended its line from Bushnell to the mouth of Hazel Creek. The company built a small depot there and gave it the name Ritter. The Ritter company then began construction of a standard-gauge railroad up Hazel Creek to its mill site at Proctor. Above Proctor they built a narrow-gauge railroad that eventually ran all the way to the cascades, two miles from the crest of the Smokies at Silers Bald, with branch lines running up

Sugar Fork, Bone Valley Creek, and Walkers Creek. On the narrow-gauge sections of its railroad, Ritter brought in geared Shay locomotives. While slower than the piston-driven engines used on standard-gauge railroads, the Shays proved more stable in the curves and able to negotiate steeper grades. The railroad was chartered as the Smoky Mountain Railway Company.

Ritter's capital investment did not stop with the railroad, however, as the company intended to process the timber on Hazel Creek before shipping it out to distant markets. At Proctor the company constructed a state-of-the-art double-band sawmill capable of processing tens of thousands of board-feet of timber every day. To further finish the rough boards that came out of the mill, they also built drying kilns, a flooring mill to convert oak, maple, and beech boards into fine strip and parquet flooring, and a planing mill to produce boards for home construction or for "dimension lumber" used in the furniture industry. As Ray Shepherd observed, the "all-inclusive" nature of the Proctor mill made it both an unusual operation and an especially profitable one for Ritter: "It would've been unique anywhere but to be on Hazel Creek and the way it was isolated was probably what's so fascinating about it to a lot of people because they had everything under one roof so to speak… That's where Ritter made his money, not in sawmilling, but by value adding the products that he sawmilled."

The isolation of Hazel Creek also meant that Ritter had to make extensive capital investments to house and provide for the needs of his workers. While Ritter provided work for locals like Granville and Seymour Calhoun, they had to import most of their skilled labor. As Ray Shepherd recalled: "He [Ritter] had the best. He, he brought people in to this area that were not native from here. For all the skilled labor, for the engineers on the trains, the sawyers, the saw-filers, his millwrights, these people… the people from Hazel Creek were merely the laborers that worked in the sawmill either packing lumber for the planing mill or working the logging crews. Even his foremen who were working the logging crews were brought in."

Proctor quickly expanded from four or five log houses in 1903 to a community of nearly 1000 inhabitants once the timber and milling operations became fully operational in the mid 1910s. The buildings in Proctor were not the typical poor-quality structures found in many timber camps or mine and textile mill villages in the South. Alice Posey recalled Proctor as "a beautiful country town." Duane Oliver asserted that the company constructed its buildings using quality lumber: "Since Ritter produced an immense amount of the finest quality lumber, the company never stinted in its use and built fine buildings of which everyone was proud and which thirty years later, were still structurally sound."

Houses in the community varied in size with most married workers' houses having two to three bedrooms and some of the houses of management being quite sizable. All of the houses had running water and eventually had both indoor plumbing and electricity. The company sited worker houses on the left side (facing upstream) of Hazel Creek along what workers dubbed Calico Street. Alice Posey commented on the appealing appearance of the housing: "All the houses were whitewashed and the fences too."

Management housing clustered across the creek along Struttin' Street. One of the most elaborate houses built in the community was one built by Orson P. Burlingame, Ritter's chief civil engineer. In 1922, after the 60-year old Burlingame married 30 year-old Lillie Lucille Brooks, a local woman who was the post mistress at Medlin, the couple built a 14-room home of "the finest lumber available." Their daughter recalled her childhood home: "The doors were made of curly poplar. The living room and dining room had beamed ceiling. Four fireplaces added cheer to these rooms and to the master bedroom. Hardwood floors were throughout the house."

Ritter also constructed several large community buildings. The central focus of the community was the large commissary building where Hazel Creek residents could buy most anything they needed. The building, located at the end of Struttin' Street, doubled as the Ritter Company offices. What workers could not buy from the commissary could now be conveniently purchased through mail order and delivered to another new building, the Proctor train depot, located next to the commissary. On the Calico Street side of Hazel Creek, the company built a large boarding house to accommodate its single workers on a hill just above the mill. Next to the boarding house, a clubhouse for visiting dignitaries—mainly executives from Ritter's home office in Columbus, Ohio—offered finer accommodations. As Ray Shepherd observed, "The clubhouse was more of the upper echelon."

Ritter located most of the buildings important to the community's social life on Calico Street. The company constructed a new Baptist church just below the clubhouse and boarding house perhaps as a subtle reminder to the mostly single residents of those buildings to watch their behavior. Downstream from the church sat the community building, the center for local recreation. The building contained pool tables and a large room for movies shown on Saturday night and a variety of community gatherings, including dances and box suppers. For several years in the 1910s, Granville Calhoun managed the facility. A café/ice cream shop was built next to the community building. Further downstream on the Stuttin' Street side, Ritter built a new school to educate the growing number of children in the community. The ballfield/playground sat behind the school in the bend in the creek where the Proctor campsite is now located.

The company built a separate community upstream from the mill known as North Proctor for African-American workers, most of whom worked in segregated crews as woodhicks. These workers were the first African Americans in the area, but little is known about their lives and the community they made on Hazel Creek.

To house the woodhicks working far upstream and on Hazel Creek tributaries, the company constructed portable "rail houses." The one-to-two room, red-painted buildings came equipped with an iron ring so a steam-powered log loader could

Shay Locomotive

**THE GEARED SHAY LOCOMOTIVE ENABLED COMPANIES LIKE RITTER
LUMBER CO. TO LOG EVEN THE MOST REMOTE SECTIONS OF THE SMOKIES.**

lift the building and place it on a flatcar to be transported and off-loaded near a
logging site. Rail houses used to accommodate single men had bunks built into the
walls. Ritter allowed foremen, saw-filers, cooks and other upper-level employees to
bring their families and their houses were set up more like a standard home. Other
portable buildings became kitchens, dining halls, wash houses, commissaries, and
post offices.

Cutting the trees, transporting them to mill, processing the timber, and then
shipping it out to market involved a lot of strenuous labor. The work began with a
team of "swampers" whose job was to clear underbrush and create skidways where
huge Percheron horses skidded—or dragged—logs to the railhead. Other workers
built wooden flumes to bring logs down steep grades or set up steam-powered
overhead skidders, cable systems used to bring logs down mountains from as far as
a mile away.

After these preparations the woodhicks with their razor-sharp crosscut saws—
known as "misery whips"—and finely honed axes took to the woods. There they
felled the giant hardwoods of Hazel Creek, trimming the branches off, and sawing
the trees into manageable lengths. Crews then prepared the timber for hauling to
the railhead by attaching chains for horses and teamsters to skid out to the end of
a flume or railhead or attached to a cable to be lifted and then winched down the
mountain.

The work was highly destructive of the forest environment as the woodhicks

Proctor Community

PROCTOR BECAME A THRIVING COMMUNITY IN THE 1910S. THE RITTER LUMBER CO. BUILT ELABORATE HOMES FOR ITS MANAGERS. WORKERS' HOMES WERE WELL CONSTRUCTED WITH RUNNING WATER AND EVENTUALLY INDOOR PLUMBING AND ELECTRICITY. RITTER ALSO BUILT A COMMISSARY, BOARDING HOUSE, CLUBHOUSE, A CHURCH, AND A SCHOOL.

cut every merchantable tree. They axed even the smaller trees for pulpwood and the falling forest giants knocked down much of what they left behind. Loggers left smaller branches, so-called "slash," on the ground which dried out creating a tin-der-box environment, highly susceptible to fire especially during dry weather. The logging also destroyed wildlife habitat and opened thin soils up for erosion and the silting of Hazel Creek and its tributaries. Horace Kephart once talked to a "northern lumberman" who admitted his company cared little for the environmental or social impact of their logging operations and employed a "cut and run" strategy: "All we want here is to get the most we can get out of this country, as quick as we can, and then get out."

Once the timber arrived at the railhead, workers used steam-powered log loaders to transfer them to railcars for transport down to the Proctor mill. The job of top loader, responsible for unhooking the huge tongs used to lift the logs onto railcars, was a particularly hazardous occupation. A Tennessee log loader once comment-ed that top loading was as "dangerous as a cocked shotgun with a drunk woman holdin' the trigger." Hauling the logs by train to the mill was no picnic either with train wrecks a common occurrence. *The Hardwood Bark*—a monthly Ritter publica-tion—recorded a humorous conversation between executive E. E. Ritter and Charlie

Wilson, an engineer on one of Ritter's trains, as they viewed the wreckage of locomotive No. 25 as it lay upside down in Hazel Creek. Ritter lamented, "Well there
lies four thousand for repairs." Wilson responded with his own lament, "Yes, and
under the engine there also lies twelve cans of Prince Albert [pipe tobacco] I just
purchased this morning." Not all such incidents ended on such a humorous note.

When the loaded trains arrived at the mill, workers dumped the logs into a pond
to wash off the dirt and facilitate grading and sorting. Clarence Vance, who worked
as a logger on Hazel Creek, recalled the skill of pond man Preacher Thurmond
Medford "who knew his logs." Medford "walked on a floating raft carrying a long
pole with spikes in the end and steered the logs one by one on to the 'jack slip' that
hauled them up into the mill." In the mill, band saws cut the logs into lumber which
workers then graded, sorted, and stacked in the lumber yard. The timber was then
air-dried for six months. The higher quality oak, maple, and beech boards went to
the drying kiln and planing mill to be made into fine flooring or processed for dimension lumber. Some of the boards that came out of the Proctor mill, particularly
ones cut from Hazel Creek's huge poplars, were as much as three-feet wide.

Ritter shipped its lumber products from the Proctor mill to distant places in the
United States and Europe. As Lance Holland observed, "the virgin timber of Hazel
Creek was processed into the finest strip and parquet flooring and shipped via their
offices in Liverpool, London, Glasgow, Antwerp, and Cologne, ultimately gracing
the floors of some of Europe's grandest buildings." Other Ritter lumber products
found their way to the North Carolina Piedmont for the burgeoning furniture
industry, and some traveled all over the nation to fuel the building boom created by
growing industrialization and World War I. In its 16-year history on Hazel Creek,
the Proctor mill produced over 166 million board feet of timber.

Working for Ritter involved a lot of danger and relatively low pay. Journalist
Vic Weals noted, "life in the logging woods in the early years of this [20th] century
was touch and go. There were so many ways to get hurt by falling timber, a flying
axe, a rolling log, the swinging tongs of a log loader, a runaway locomotive on a
steep railroad grade, a kicking logging horse, or even ornery 'white mule' [moon-
shine] on Saturday night." Ritter's company doctor was a busy man. According
to Duane Oliver, to face these dangers, the average Ritter worker made about
sixty-five cents a day for a ten-to-twelve hour work day, and a six-day work week,
although this increased to a dollar a day, and more, in the later 1910s and 1920s.

For most of Ritter's Hazel Creek workers, however, the risks and low pay were
worth the rewards. Wages are a relative measure, and for many of Ritter's workers
the pay was much more than they could make farming their marginal land. In addition, Ritter paid in cash, not in scrip as many other lumber companies in the Smokies did, and the workers could spend their wages wherever they liked. Seymour
Calhoun, who worked as a water boy for a crew of African-American woodhicks,
recalled his perception of the pay he received as a fourteen-year old boy: "I went to

work 14, when I was 14 years old... Got a big pay, 50 cents a day when I worked 10 hours good. Walked anywhere from a mile to 3 miles to make it. But, when the end of the month come I had 7 or 8 dollars, and that was a lot of money in them days, for a boy anyway."

Working for Ritter also had other benefits as the company seemed to have a relatively paternalistic attitude about its workers. Many of its employees, in the words of historian Stephen Taylor, "remembered W. M. Ritter as a benevolent employer who genuinely cared about the people who worked for him." Clarence Vance put it succinctly, "We felt like a family." The company often rewarded its workers when they exceeded production goals. *The Hardwood Bark* reported on the fine showing of Ritter's Hazel Creek workers in October 1922, even in the midst of some significant changes in its operations, and the subsequent reward that came to workers: "With a cut of over 30,000 feet and shipments of over 400,000 and October not yet ended... it is very apparent that the changes have not impaired our efficiency, and we all took Saturday afternoon off again this month, with pay to all full time men."

One of the benefits that many folks on Hazel Creek enjoyed in the Ritter era was the services of a company doctor. For much of that era, Dr. J. G. Storie filled the position. An article in the North Shore Historical Association newsletter, *Fontana*, described the good doctor: "He was doctor and friend to everyone on the creek. He delivered babies, stitched up their cuts, bandaged their bruises; you name it. He was on hand wherever he was needed." Doc Storie made regular rounds up and down Hazel Creek riding on what he called "my speeder," a bicycle-like contraption with four wheels that ran on the railroad tracks. The train pulled his speeder up stream in the morning and then Storie coasted back to Proctor making visits along the way. For Storie's medical services, single men paid $1.00 a month and families $1.50. In 1922 *The Hardwood Bark* did a piece on Storie and asserted, "We are willing to wager that he is the most popular man on the Creek, particularly among the ladies." The article further reported that between his arrival in 1912 to 1922, Storie "officiated at the births of 685 babies."

Storie's successor, Dr. Riter, also proved popular with the community, especially when he purchased the first radio on the creek and opened his office up in the evenings for folks to listen to their favorite serials or music programs. In 1924, *The Hardwood Bark* reported, "Every evening numbers of people can be seen going to Dr. Riter's office. No, there isn't any epidemic of any kind in Proctor now (unless it's radio fever). Dr. Riter has a radio installed in his office and invites everyone to hear it. The office is crowded every evening."

While Hazel Creek had had schools for a number of years, the coming of Ritter greatly improved both the quality and quantity of education in the community. In 1914, Ritter built a new four-room school at Proctor. In 1923, *The Hardwood Bark* reported that in the previous year, probably the school's peak year, the Proctor School enrolled 138 students with an average attendance of 121. Both Ritter and

Proctor School

THE FOUR-ROOM PROCTOR SCHOOL, BUILT BY RITTER, SERVED NOT ONLY
AS THE COMMUNITY'S EDUCATION CENTER, BUT ALSO HOSTED IMPORTANT
COMMUNITY EVENTS SUCH AS PLAYS AND BOX SUPPERS.

the community itself supplemented the county school appropriation to provide a
modern, well-equipped school. *The Hardwood Bark* reporter claimed, "If our school
doesn't acquire all of the fixin's that most city schools have, it won't be for lack
of effort on the part of the faculty and pupils. First, it was a play which ran two
successful nights, and next it was a box supper, both of which netted good returns
with which to purchase some extra school equipment." The coming of the railroad
also allowed the school to have competitive sports teams; basketball and baseball
for boys and basketball for girls. *The Hardwood Bark* reported on one interscho-
lastic contest in 1922 when the "Proctor Basket Ball Girls played a dashing game
against Almond High at Bryson City, score 16 to 9 in favor of the Proctor team."
The increased population of the Ritter era also allowed for smaller schools, at least
temporarily, at Cable Branch, Medlin, Camp Seven, Walkers Creek, Proctor Creek,
and Sugar Fork.

Ritter's Community Club provided additional social and cultural outlets for Hazel Creekers. Each Saturday, the Community Club theater, which seated 200 - 300
people, filled both its evening movie showings. Granville Calhoun, who ran the club
from 1913 to 1916, recalled those silent movie days and particularly the brittleness
of the films: "There was always a lot of trouble with the film breaking. I had me
a Negro family from over at Franklin that made music when the film broke and
while it was being repaired." After the movie showings, the patrons moved chairs
aside for dancing. The Community Club also had a number of pool tables, "busy

Planing Room

RITTER CONSTRUCTED A STATE-OF-THE-ART DOUBLE-BAND SAWMILL CAPABLE OF PROCESSING TENS OF THOUSANDS OF BOARD FEET OF TIMBER EVERY DAY. THEY ALSO BUILT DRYING KILNS, A FLOORING MILL TO CONVERT OAK, MAPLE, AND BEECH BOARDS INTO FINE STRIP AND PARQUET FLOORING, AND A PLANING MILL TO PRODUCE BOARDS FOR HOME CONSTRUCTION OR FOR "DIMENSION LUMBER" USED IN THE FURNITURE INDUSTRY.

every evening from the time the place opens until the lights go out," and its Athletic Branch sponsored a baseball team and even constructed a community tennis court "garbed in the latest fashions of nets and racquets." The Educational Branch of the Community Club organized a Literary Society that held lectures and, at least on one occasion, a "mock trial" of local character Dinty Moore for drunk and disorderly conduct. As *The Hardwood Bark* reported, "Despite the valiant efforts of his attorneys…, Dinty was found guilty and sentenced to ride the rail as long as the fellows were willing to carry it. Dinty says he wouldn't have minded being convicted if only they had not convinced his 'better half' that the charges were true."

Ritter also brought community-wide holiday celebrations to Hazel Creek for the first time. The company declared a holiday on July 4 and held a major event at the Proctor School ball field complete with watermelon, ice cream, a variety of track and field competitions, baseball games, carnival, and the ever-popular greasy pole climb. Easter Sunday brought a company-sponsored Easter egg hunt for the children and other activities. The community also gathered on Halloween for a play, box supper, and "prettiest girl" and "ugliest man" contests. Weddings also became occasions for impromptu holiday-like celebrations. Revelers generally treated the wedding couple to the old tradition of the charivari—better known as a "shivaree" in Hazel Creek. As Clarence Vance remembered this tradition, "A large group would get together in the night and we went marching to the home of the bride and groom. Two of the fellows carried a large circular saw on an iron bar and another would beat it with a hammer as we walked along." When the crowd arrived at the couple's home, they placed the bride in a red wagon and pulled her around as they paraded the groom on a rail.

For many Hazel Creek residents, Christmas was the high point of the year and both the community and the Ritter company went all out in its celebration. The company put up a huge Christmas tree at the Proctor Baptist Church and the church held a large community program on Christmas Eve. *The Hardwood Bark* described one such program in 1924: "The girls of the Junior B. Y. P. U. [Baptist Young Peoples Union] rendered a nice program, after which the exercises were turned over to Mr. and Mrs. Santa Claus who delighted the kiddies very much by passing around among them and distributing handfuls of candy." The company also provided every child under the age of 14 with an individual Christmas gift and, as Duane Oliver recalled, a "bag of apples, oranges, nuts and candy." For those who could not make it to Proctor, the company sent one of its Shay locomotives up the creek delivering toys and candy to the children in the more remote lumber camps, something the engineers and railroad crews enjoyed almost as much as the children.

The residents of Hazel Creek also enjoyed a richer religious life with the coming of Ritter. The options remained Baptist or Baptist, but churches held services and special events much more frequently. The company built a sanctuary for the Proctor Baptist Church, the first, and only, congregation on Hazel Creek to have its own church building and not meet in a school. The church building was two stories tall, painted white, and paneled on the inside, according to Alice Posey, with "fine-dressed varnish strips." Access to the meeting room on the second floor, which doubled as the Odd Fellows Hall, was by steps on the outside of the building. While church had generally consisted of once or twice monthly preaching prior to the Ritter era, the Proctor Baptist Church offered weekly preaching, Sunday School, B.Y.P.U for young people on Sunday evenings, and Wednesday prayer meetings.

Besides regular church services, the residents of Hazel Creek also actively participated in other religious events. Church revivals remained important community events and with the increased population, became even larger. Itinerant evangelists also came to the community in the 1920s with large tents usually pitched in a field in North Proctor. Singing was always an important part of church life on Hazel Creek, but with improved access the area became a regular stopping point on the circuits of shape-note music teachers and their week-long singing schools. In addition, the Proctor Church held an "All-Day-Singing-Dinner-on-the-Ground" event on a Sunday every summer. As Duane Oliver recalled, "People from all around gathered at Proctor, listened to quartets and choirs from various churches, and then stuffed themselves with food brought by all the housewives, and then listened to some more singing."

Decoration Days held at local cemeteries in late spring or early fall were another important annual event with religious connotations. The festivities began early in the week before the "decoration" with women gathering to make flowers out of crepe paper using patterns passed down for generations. The women then attached wire to the flowers for affixing to headstones. Some dipped their flowers in paraffin to help them last longer. Men gathered at the cemetery on Saturday with shovels and hoes to, in the words of Duane Oliver, "chop all the weeds, straighten up the leaning gravestones and neatly mound up each grave." On Sunday, those with kin in a particular cemetery gathered there to place the flowers on the graves, hear a short sermon, sing some songs, enjoy dinner on the ground, and reminisce about their ancestors.

The *Hardwood Bark* also reported on other pastimes enjoyed by folks on Hazel Creek. A reporter commented in 1923, "After a summer spent in comparative quietness, we seem to have gone picnic wild in September. There have been picnics almost too numerous to mention, but practically everyone on Hazel Creek has been on at least one picnic this month. The 'fryers' are getting scarce." In May 1924, the newsletter reported that Jack Bryant and Marl Culbertson went on a two-day expedition combining fishing and gathering. "We were unable to learn just how many fish they caught, but we can certainly say that they ate at least one 'ramp' each." Clarence Vance recalled the impromptu events organized by the young people of the community including ice-skating on the mill pond, parties at individual homes, and bonfires on the ball field where Wallace Swann brought his guitar and led a sing-a-long. Vance remembered, "The social life of our town during those years was something to be remembered."

By the mid-1920s, Hazel Creek had become quite modern in some respects. Although a drivable road from Bushnell to Hazel Creek would not be finished until the spring of 1925, *The Hardwood Bark* counted six automobiles in Proctor in October 1924. Ritter mill employees Ed Matthews and Joe Swann had, on the side, even gone into the used car business to supply the growing demand. With this improved access and a road under construction over Deals Gap into Tennessee, folks in the community touted the arrival of a new industry, tourism. *The Hardwood Bark* in May 1925, reported, "Work on the new Highway is progressing rapidly and we are glad to see the road now open for traffic, many tourists passing through daily… Arrangements have been made to have the yard around the Hazel Creek store improved in order to allow the cars parking space."

Despite the new prosperity and optimism about Hazel Creek's future, it was all too apparent that the long boom of the Ritter era was about to bust. By 1925, Ritter had "cut out" the Hazel Creek watershed and would soon cut out for new forests elsewhere. Even after the company announced it had sold most of its land on Hazel Creek to Asheville, North Carolina developer Jim Stikeleather and his partner George Smathers, who planned to log the still untapped upper reaches of Bone Valley and use the rest for an exclusive hunting and fishing club, the local Hazel Creek correspondent remained optimistic about the area's future: "Since the purchase of this property by a realty company in Asheville, North Carolina, we understand that Proctor will be known as the 'Smoky Mountain Tourist City' after the W. M. Ritter Lumber Company has completed operations."

In 1926, all of Ritter's operations dramatically slowed. The company laid off workers or transferred them to other Ritter sites, pulled up the railroad tracks, moved out the trains, and the once thriving and vibrant town of Proctor became a virtual ghost town. On August 26, 1926, the planing mill produced its last piece of flooring and shut down forever at 4:00 p.m. Workers tore down much of the mill complex—except for buildings made of concrete and brick, which still stand in spooky ruin—along with most of the workers' housing, including the boarding house. The company sold the lumber used to construct these structures and the purchasers built many fine homes with it in the region. A few community buildings did remain standing including the clubhouse, the school, the church, and the train depot. Several of the larger houses on Struttin' Street built for Ritter management remained and Granville Calhoun purchased the community building and turned it into a store.

Those whose families had spent generations on Hazel Creek now had a chance to reflect on the Ritter boom years and the impact of that era on their economic life, their social life, and the environment. The loss of Ritter's jobs was devastating as the people had become so accustomed to life in an industrial/cash-based economy and could not imagine a return to subsistence agriculture. As Duane Oliver observed, "No one wanted to or could return to the old 19th century subsistence level, and that was no longer possible anyway. Sufficient cash from a steady income and what it could buy had become too appealing as a way of life…" Generally speaking, to secure a cash income they would have to go elsewhere. As they said their good-byes to homesites, family cemeteries, churches, and schools that meant so much to them, they might have looked at what Ritter had brought, and had taken, with new eyes. As Ray Shepherd observed: "And of course even people in this area were a little mixed, I think, with Ritter sawmill. They wanted to see some jobs and opportunities but when they got back up on the ridges and looked back down, the common term was, they've skint that thing like a bar. Just really they'd skinned the land."

CHAPTER FOUR

Bust Times

$\mathcal{T}$he families who remained on Hazel Creek after Ritter shut down its operations faced few viable options. Some were able to pull scraps together to re-
sume a "patchwork quilt" existence—farming some, cutting acid wood for tanneries
and pulp wood for paper plants, and combing the denuded hills for medicinal herbs,
particularly ginseng, to sell in nearby markets. Others tried to take advantage of
improved transportation and tap into the growing tourism industry. The only thing
in the immediate area that even closely approximated the experience of working
for Ritter and the steady cash wages it supplied was the new copper mine being
developed a little over four miles away on Eagle Creek. For most people, however,
their chief viable alternative was to move away and seek industrial employment
elsewhere. Indeed, as Don Casada observed, the number of people who left Hazel
Creek between 1930 to 1940 far exceeded the number of individuals later removed
when the Tennessee Valley Authority built the Fontana Dam.

Attempts to develop the so-called Fontana mine began as early as 1924 under
the auspices of the Montvale Lumber Co., but their early efforts got off to a less
than auspicious start. A report of the North Carolina Department of Labor gives an
account of an investigation into the deaths of two miners, F. W. McGuire and Wil-
burn Crisp, on July 14, 1924. Bryson City pharmacist and civic leader Kelly Ben-
nett conducted an inquest at the request of the Commissioner of Labor and attribut-
ed the "disaster" to "negligence and carelessness on the part of the two deceased
men." It is not known if this accident prompted Montvale to cease operations, but

Miners

EAGLE CREEK MINERS BERT AND HENRY DAVIS, 1929.

most of the development of the mine and its facilities came two years later.

In 1926, a group of investors, including Ritter Lumber Co. doctor J. F. Riter, associated with the Ducktown Chemical and Iron Co. of nearby southeast Tennessee purchased a lease from the Montvale Lumber Co. for a little over 2000 acres to exploit the copper ore under the ground. The mine operated from March 1926 to January 1944, produced 529,350 tons of ore that, according to a U. S. Geological

Survey report, averaged "7% copper, 2% zinc, 14 g/t [grams per ton] silver, and .28 g/t gold." Miners dug a series of vertical shafts to access the ore body going almost 1600 feet underground. At its peak in 1931, the mine employed over 300 people, although for much of the 1930s and '40s it employed about 50 miners. The ore was shipped by train to Isabella, Tennessee for processing. While the mine supplied some Hazel Creek residents with income, it also subjected them to the ongoing boom and bust cycles of resource extraction.

The completion of a road to Hazel Creek by the Forney Creek Road District not long before Ritter pulled up its tracks and moved on did create some limited economic possibilities for those who wanted to stay. Indeed, Hazel Creek became better known for other natural resources, its bear and trout, during the 1930s than for its timber and copper. Hazel Creek had long had a reputation as a haven for bear hunters and trout fishermen, but with the acquisition of much of Ritter's land by Asheville businessmen Jim Stikeleather and George Smathers and their creation of the elite Hazel Creek Hunting & Fishing Club, the area took on mythical status for its big bear and big trout.

Somehow, both the trout and bear populations had survived the "skinning" that the land took under Ritter's land management. From the days of Ziegler and Grosscup's *Heart of the Alleghenies*, Hazel Creek was known for its thriving population of native speckled trout. That population had been devastated by the splash dam logging conducted by Taylor & Crate in the late 19th century. Trout did begin to come back in the 1910s and Granville Calhoun stocked the stream in 1919 with rainbow trout procured from a U.S. government hatchery in Tennessee. The rainbows soon began to thrive in the creek, much to the detriment of the smaller brook trout who were either consumed or consigned to the upper reaches of Hazel Creek and its tributaries. During the Ritter days, both Hazel Creek workers and company executives on junkets from company headquarters in Ohio enjoyed fishing the creek and its reputation for big trout spread further.

When Stikeleather took over, he hired Granville Calhoun as manager and a pair of wardens, local bear-hunting legends Jim Laws and his son Oliver, to watch over the land and the creek and to keep locals from poaching the bear and fish and continued to stock the streams with big trout. Stikeleather's dream was to make Hazel Creek a strictly fly-fishing stream although with over 30 miles of streams, and needing the goodwill of locals, that proved difficult. Soon, however, outdoor writers lauded Hazel Creek as one of the premier trout fishing streams in the nation. Outdoor writer Jim Gasque wrote in his classic book *Hunting and Fishing in the Great Smoky Mountains*: "As dry-fly water, Hazel ranks at the very top. Few good dry-fly men have been defeated during late May or in June, July, and August." Years later, journalist John Parris eloquently described the sentiments of many who fished Hazel during this time period: "It's the kind of trout water that makes a man whistle through his teeth, and its fishing is enough to make a man fall to his knees in a silent prayer of thanksgiving."

Horace Kephart's, and other writers', vivid descriptions of Hazel Creek bear hunts in *Our Southern Highlanders*, national outdoor magazines, and newspapers also gave the area legendary status for its big bear. Stories about Hazel Creek residents' bear-killing prowess spread far and wide. Calhoun claimed to have killed three bears in one day and was credited with killing perhaps the biggest bear ever in the Smokies, which weighed over 600 pounds. "The scales we had only drug 500 pounds and the scales hit the top mark and almost broke." A 1931 *Asheville Citizen* story recounted the hunt for "Battling Sam," a huge bear who frequented Bone Valley and was known as a cattle and sheep killer. When hunters brought Sam to heel, and "even after being shot repeatedly," the bear still mustered the strength "to slap 'Old Boss,' a noted bear dog, as he rushed by him, the dog being knocked 15 feet in the air." The bear's hide measured 10 feet, eight inches nose to tail and weighed "at least 600 pounds."

To house their guests—which included notable businessmen, writers, politicians, and sports figures including Branch Rickey, President of the St. Louis Cardinals and later the Brooklyn Dodgers, hall of fame pitcher Jay "Dizzy" Dean, famous outdoor writer John Taintor Foote, Houghton Mifflin director and noted author Ferris Greenslet, and New Jersey U.S. Senator William Smathers—Stikeleather built a rough cabin near the confluence of the Little Tennessee River and Hazel Creek. More commonly, however, the club used the old Ritter Clubhouse for guests and Granville Calhoun remodeled a room on the second floor of the old Ritter community building that he had converted into a store to give the hunters and fishermen closer access to their quarry.

Stikeleather hired cooks, guides, and dog handlers to serve his guests. The guides and dog handlers for the bear hunts constituted what writer Bob Plott called "a mountain bear hunters hall of fame." Heading the list were locals Jim Laws, his son Oliver, Bill Wiggins, and Wince Cable. Stikeleather also called in Haywood County legend Von Plott, who brought his equally legendary pack of Plott hounds—a breed the Plott family developed especially for bear and boar hunting and now the state dog of North Carolina—over for big hunts. Oliver Laws recalled those hunts to Bob Plott: "Me, my daddy [Jim] and the Plotts were on all the bear hunts up there—we didn't miss any. And we knew everything they was to know about bears. We knew the day before what a bear was going to do that night. My daddy and me and Von and Little George Plott were the runningest hunters I have ever seen."

On occasions, Stikeleather brought in Uncle Mark Cathey, a legend as both a trout fisherman and bear hunter from Deep Creek on the east side of Swain County. Cathey's gun rack had 53 "bear notches" cut into it by his death in 1944, several of those taken on Hazel Creek. Cathey, however, was best known for his unique and unorthodox style of dry-fly fishing where he "danced" the fly across the water to en-

Fonze Cable

FONZE CABLE DISPLAYS BEAR HIDE TAKEN IN A HAZEL CREEK HUNT.

tice the trout. Jim Gasque described one of Cathey's performances on Hazel Creek witnessed by Jim Stikeleather and Captain R. D. Gatewood:

> The two men stood and witnessed one of old Mark's greatest performances. Mark danced the fly back and forth on the side of the rock where the trout was hiding. The fish was aware of the presence of man, but the fly danced with such cunning the trout just couldn't resist it. He was weakening—two or three times he darted from his rock toward the fly, only to turn back to his hiding-place without taking. "Just keep watching him Captain," Mark said. "I'm gonna aggravate him till he'll forget me; then he'll fasten on." And he

The Proctor CCC Camp

THE PROCTOR CCC CAMP HELPED ALLEVIATE SOME OF THE STRESS OF THE
GREAT DEPRESSION FOR HAZEL CREEK. THE CAMP PROVIDED EMPLOYMENT,
EDUCATION AND VOCATIONAL TRAINING OPPORTUNITIES FOR A NUMBER OF LOCAL
MEN, PROVIDED A MARKET FOR LOCAL PRODUCE, AND EVEN ENLIVENED THE AREA'S
SOCIAL LIFE.

was right. After several darts out and back, the fish finally abandoned all
caution and took that fly.

Other Stikeleather guests had equally unforgettable experiences on Hazel Creek.
Branch Rickey was a frequent visitor to Hazel Creek for bear hunts and on one
memorable three-day hunt in the early 1940s personally killed two bears with his
L. C. Smith, 12-gauge, double-barrel shotgun. After a 1935 hunt, Rickey wrote a
letter—transcribed in Bob Plott's book *Colorful Characters of the Great Smoky
Mountains*—to Von Plott praising the mountain legend's abilities as a dog-handler,
hunter, and for his sheer athleticism: "I shall never forget your ability to run as fast
as those dogs, or just about as fast. Everyone agrees that you ran more than twelve
miles that morning up and down those mountains; and at every crossing and across
every hillcrest you were never seen to be walking—you were always running. You
are what I call a finished hunter. And I think I would rather go hunting with you in
charge of the dogs than anyone else in the world."

The Stikeleather operation proved so successful that it attracted both competi-
tors and the beginnings of a second home industry. In 1933, an article in the *Asheville Citizen* announced that Granville Calhoun had gone out on his own and created

a fishing camp on "six miles of well stocked streams in virgin fishing territory." Calhoun advertised "accommodations for forty or fifty at a time," but details of the long-term success of his operation are sketchy. Junkets to the Hazel Creek Fishing Club also prompted members of the Kress family to purchase land in Bone Valley from the Hall family and build a hunting and fishing lodge. Phillip Rust, a Delaware businessman, also purchased 4500 acres in the upper reaches of nearby Forney Creek where, according to historian Stephen Taylor, he created a "private retreat and preserve." On his tract he practiced modern forest and wildlife management techniques hiring four wardens to oversee the property and constructing a nursery, a trout hatchery, and thirty miles of hiking trails that connected to the newly created Great Smoky Mountains National Park trail system. He also built a small hydroelectric power plant to provide electricity to his house, garages, barns, and nursery.

However, these elite facilities provided little in the way of relief for Hazel Creek residents faced with few options for cash and a faltering national economy during the Great Depression. Some relief did come, especially to young men, when the New Deal brought a Civilian Conservation Corps camp to Proctor at the site once occupied by the Ritter lumberyard. CCC camps provided employment to young men aged 17 - 28—and some older men, known as Local Experienced Men or L. E. M.s who served as supervisors—working in national parks, national forests, and state parks to conserve natural resources. The National Park Service managed the Proctor camp (NP-23) and worked to support the newly created Great Smoky Mountains National Park. Enrollees replanted trees in areas, such as Hazel Creek, devastated by clear cutting, improved roads and bridges, built hiking and fire trails into the park, constructed and staffed fire towers, and fought fires.

The CCC camp offered a needed boon to Hazel Creek residents providing employment for young men (although enrollees came from all over the eastern U.S.) and L. E. M.s, providing a market for local farmers' produce, and even enlivening local social life. Duane Oliver observed that the CCC enrollees were "well integrated with the life of the community." For CCC enrollee Kermit Anderson, "Proctor was like a second home. At Proctor we had very good relations with the local people [not always the case] and were welcomed to, and participated in, most community functions such as church and school." Indeed, some Hazel Creek residents were especially "welcoming" to the CCC boys as both Oliver and Anderson reported that several enrollees "married local girls."

Like most things in Hazel Creek, however, the CCC boom went bust pretty quickly and by the late 1930s, the local economy and social life offered few opportunities or enticements for young people. Once again outside observers captured an image of the region and its people for a national audience at the very bottom of a bust period. Of course this did not stop folks from characterizing life in the area as isolated and backward. Indeed, by this point, Horace Kephart's version of life in the region presented in *Our Southern Highlanders* had become gospel among most educated Americans. This time the outsiders were employees of the Federal Writers Project, a division of the Works Progress Administration (WPA), who traveled the nation collecting information for a series of guides to the various states. The 1939 WPA publication *North Carolina: A Guide to the Old North State*, recounts these observations after a visit to Bushnell:

> Their [the original white inhabitants] descendants have preserved to a marked degree the individualism, independence, and originality of character of their ancestors. Although in the popular concept every mountaineer uses hillbilly dialect and handles both bullets and ballads with an Elizabethan abandon and a free frontier fervor, valley-dwelling mountaineers are not so different from lowlanders as they are from the isolated inhabitants of the coves far back in the mountains. Pungent, graphic, and expressive, the deep-cove type coins his own word if he can think of none at the moment that suits his need. Though the Scotch-Irish influence is noticeable chiefly in the sounding of the letter r, the English is really predominant. He speaks often in Elizabethan, Chaucerian, or pre-Chaucerian idiom; his pronoun hit antedates English itself, while Ey God, a favorite expletive, is the original of egad and precedes Chaucer. The highlander uses many expressions in common with the Canterbury Tales: heap o' Jol\s, afore, peart; some of his ballets are old English folk songs.

Developments on the heels of the publication of the WPA guide, however, provided dramatic evidence that life and culture in the Hazel Creek area was shaped much more by modern forces than it was locked in "Elizabethan, Chaucerian, or pre-Chaucerian idiom."

In 1941, Hazel Creek began its third boom period in less than fifty years when the Tennessee Valley Authority's massive Fontana Dam project arrived on its doorstep. Indeed, the coming of World War II helped produce a boom in the local job market that even dwarfed the heyday of the Ritter Lumber Co. In addition to the TVA project, war demand led the owners of the Fontana copper mine to dramatically increase production. According to Duane Oliver, the company "was running three full shifts." Even the Adams mine on Sugar Fork, which had not operated since 1900 due to the lingering litigation between Adams and Westfeldt and low demand in the copper market, resumed operation. Almost overnight, the problems for Hazel Creek residents became overcrowding and inflation rather than loss of population and depression.

The Fontana Dam project had its roots in the early years of the 20th century when the Aluminum Company of America (Alcoa), which constructed a massive plant in East Tennessee near Maryville, began purchasing land along the Little Tennessee River to build dams to generate hydroelectric power to supply the massive need for electricity in the aluminum production process. By 1919, the company

Fontana Dam Construction

THIS MASSIVE DAM WAS COMPLETED IN LESS THAN THREE YEARS AND
PRODUCED ONE OF THE LARGEST, AND SHORTEST LIVED, ECONOMIC BOOMS
EVER ON HAZEL CREEK. IT ALSO INDIRECTLY LED TO THE DEMISE OF THE
COMMUNITY WHEN THE WATERS OF FONTANA LAKE COVERED THE ONLY
ACCESS ROAD TO THE AREA.

completed the Cheoah Dam on the Little Tennessee—famous as the backdrop for
the filming of an iconic scene in the Harrison Ford 1993 movie, "The Fugitive"—
and by 1928 the Santeetlah Dam on the Cheoah River was completed. The prize
dam site for Alcoa, however, was a site near the Fontana Mine but with the coming
of the Great Depression, the company put plans for construction on hold.

By the late 1930s, however, TVA leaders A. E. Morgan and David Lilienthal
coveted the site as well. As Stephen Taylor observed, "the narrow, deep valley
of the Little Tennessee [at Fontana] could provide a great deal of water storage,
which the agency could use to guarantee a steady supply of hydropower during the
dry season and control the usual spring floods in the Tennessee and lower Little
Tennessee Valleys, especially at Chattanooga." In 1941, with war looming and the
U.S. already ramping up its industrial production to support the British, Lilienthal
forced Alcoa to sell the 15,000 acres it had acquired in the Fontana area. In return,
TVA guaranteed that it would supply up to 20% of the East Tennessee Alcoa plant's
power needs.

Preparations for the construction of the massive dam—the tallest dam in the
eastern U.S. and at the time of its construction the fourth largest in the world—soon

Fontana Dam Construction

AT THE TIME, FONTANA WAS THE TALLEST DAM IN THE EASTERN U.S. AND THE
FOURTH LARGEST IN THE WORLD. IT WOULD SUPPLY 20% OF THE POWER FOR ALCOA
ALUMINUM, WHICH WAS DESPERATELY NEEDED FOR THE WAR EFFORT, AND UNBE-
KNOWNST TO THE GENERAL POPULATION AND HAZEL CREEK RESIDENTS IN PARTICU-
LAR, THE MANHATTAN PROJECT IN THE SECRET CITY OF OAK RIDGE.

began and job-seekers poured into the area to supply the estimated 5,000 to 7,000
workers. In addition to building a dam, the location of the site so far away from
major transportation, communication, and housing facilities meant that TVA also
needed to take on a massive road improvement project, build a railroad spur, run
hundreds of miles of telephone cable, build worker housing, mess halls, medical
facilities, recreation facilities, and even schools. The work took on new urgency
after Pearl Harbor and signs urging workers to do their patriotic duty sprang up on
the site. The most popular sign read:

> We Are Building This Dam
> To Make the Power
> To Roll the Aluminum
> To Build the Bombers
> To Beat the Bastards

Amazingly, TVA workers poured the first concrete in January 1942 and closed
the spillways in November 1944 completing the dam in less than three years. In the
process, the Hazel Creek area once again, but in even more dramatic and sudden fashion, boomed. Historian Stephen Taylor noted in *The New South's New Frontier* the
similarities and differences between this new boom and previous ones in the area:

The pressures of the coming war made it possible to build Fontana Dam. The pressures of a nation at war dictated the way in which it would be built, the type of workers to be hired, where those workers would live, what they would eat, of how they would be entertained, and even how their children would be schooled. On the surface, that seems like dramatic transformation. Yet, in reality the war superimposed a new type of temporary employment on an economy that was already structured around temporary employment. It superimposed a paternalistic management style and a company-town organization upon a people who had experienced such paternalism before, and some of the people longed for it. It brought large amounts of cash into a region filled with residents for whom cash was associated with luxury they desperately wanted… It brought more money than any previous extractive industry, but it was certainly not the first experience these people had with a cash economy. It brought more dislocation than previous industries, but it did not destroy a static civilization… As far as residents of the area were concerned, only the scale was different. Fontana in the 1940s was a boomtown, just as Proctor and Bushnell had been thirty years earlier.

Euphoria over the jobs and cash that this new massive project would bring, however, was quickly dampened as long-time residents of Hazel Creek became aware of the fact that the completion of the dam and the closing of the spillways would spell the end of their community. Folks who lived near the Little Tennessee River knew that their land would be flooded by the rising waters, but those who lived well up Hazel Creek and its tributaries soon learned that they would have to move as well. While the waters of Fontana Lake would not come near their homes, and in most cases would be miles away, the lake would submerge much of NC Highway 288, the only road connecting the community to the outside world. In the judgment of TVA—recorded in its 1950 official assessment, "The Fontana Project"—maintaining Hazel Creek's connection to Bryson City and the world would have required "an almost complete relocation" of the road. The report continued with a dispassionate bureaucratic tone: "Because of the rugged terrain the cost of replacement would have been excessive, considerably more than the value of the land served…Furthermore, the TVA was informally advised by the War Production Board that reconstruction of the road was not of sufficient importance to justify the expenditure of materials and manpower required for the work."

For TVA the solution to the road problem was simple; purchase the approximately 44,000 acres of land between the north shore of the lake and the border with the Great Smoky Mountains National Park, donate the land to the Park, and remove the people. TVA, the Department of Interior, the State of North Carolina, and Swain County did sign an agreement where the Park Service agreed to construct a road "extending from the east limit of the area to be acquired to a connection with the access road to Fontana Dam…" The State of North Carolina promised to construct a "highway connecting the proposed park road with U.S. Highway No. 19 at Bryson City…"

Most TVA officials saw no downside to this approach and viewed themselves as actually helping a backward and impoverished people enter a modern, and more prosperous, world. As Stephen Taylor observed, "TVA employed people from different backgrounds in management positions. Their attitudes toward local residents ranged from sympathy to contempt, but all shared a sense that the area's past proved its people's inability to take care of themselves." Reports from TVA's ominously named Population Readjustment Division, tasked with helping area residents relocate, reflected these attitudes. Head of the division Rome Sharp derided the "clannish attitude of the natives" and asserted that Proctor presented "a unique picture of community decadence and disorganization." Although he was a local himself, Arnold Hyde claimed that the removal of communities on the north shore of Fontana would actually help the people. "The changes brought about by the program of the Authority have offered new opportunities to dissatisfied families who realize the futility of the struggle with poverty in their present environment. The individual will not only be freed from restricted circumstances, but the community as a whole will profit by the advantages afforded by the creation of Fontana Lake."

The news that they would lose their homes and be forced to move produced a variety of reactions from Hazel Creek residents. Duane Oliver observed, "Many people looked forward to getting out in the civilized world. My father did not want to move, but my mother and grandmother were delighted to leave." Others determined to hold on and resisted selling their property, but TVA stacked the deck against them with the government's power to condemn their property under the law of eminent domain and a streamlined process of land acquisition developed over ten years of acquiring thousands of acres in the region for a number of other TVA. dams and reservoirs. Besides, fighting a TVA condemnation order in court required financial resources few Hazel Creek residents possessed.

Most area residents accepted the government's price for their land and prepared to leave. According to Duane Oliver, only a little more than 3% of Hazel Creek residents forced the government to condemn their land. Ironically, one of those who resisted was Oliver's grandmother Sadie Welch Farley who did not want to sell the family cemetery, the oldest in the area and the final resting place of Moses Proctor. TVA eventually forced her to sell for $50.

TVA assessed the property at its market rate. For the rural mountain acreage of Hazel Creek denuded of its timber, with modest homes and barns, little arable bottom land, little access to communication and transportation lines, and little or no value to tourist developers or second home owners the market value amounted to an average of $37.76 per acre. In "The Fontana Project," TVA defended the price that it admitted was "one of the lowest for any reservoir acquired to date" due to the area's

Fontana Dam

THE FONTANA PROJECT PROVIDED NEW OPPORTUNITIES FOR WORKERS AND THEIR
FAMILIES. HERE A GROUP OF THIRD GRADERS WORK ON PROJECTS IN A GREENHOUSE
AT FONTANA SCHOOL.

"mountainous character and remoteness of the reservoir setting."

As a market rate for the land, it was probably fair, but a number of people
have forcefully argued that TVA should have taken more than the market rate into
account. Larry Vickery asserted that the prices given might have been fair if folks
had been able to stay in the Hazel Creek area, but, of course, they were not. Area
residents now had to buy homes and property in places where land was much more
expensive. Vickery recounted the story of one farmer who owned twenty-eight acres
and received $8,000 - $10,000 for his property. "[W]hen he got down to Merryville
[sic] or to Knoxville, he couldn't hardly buy a building lot with that amount of money because land prices were different."

Market rate also did not take into account the emotional impact of being forcibly
removed from land that had been in families for generations. As Vickery observed:
"…if you're talking about a person's property that's been in a family for generation
after generation, that's been in a family for over a hundred years, the term 'fair market value' has no meaning. It has no bearing on a case whatsoever. We're not just
talking about dirt and trees. We're talking about lives and history." Glenn Cardwell,
a former Great Smoky Mountains National Park ranger whose family was removed

from the Greenbrier section of the park in Tennessee, commented eloquently on the emotional impact of the loss of community: "You can buy a farm anywhere, but tearing up your community does something to your spirit."

Not everyone lost their land on the north shore of Fontana Lake. The North Carolina Exploration Co. (later Cities Services Co.) who now owned the copper-rich lands around the mouth of Eagle Creek and the Adams mine on Sugar Fork failed to come to agreement with TVA on the value of its lands. TVA and the National Park Service decided to leave the 2,343.7 acres as an inholding, a fact that would later haunt the Park Service as poachers used the land as a convenient inroad into park land.

With the spillways of Fontana Dam closing in November 1944, residents had to pack up their things and get out before the rising waters inundated NC Highway 288. Many dismantled their homes, particularly those built during the Ritter era, and hauled out the high-quality lumber. Duane Oliver, his father, and cousin Edward Farley dismantled several homes near the mining town of Fontana, loaded them on railcars, shipped them to neighboring Haywood County, and built a house, still occupied by family, in Hazelwood. TVA burned whatever was left behind. Duane Oliver recalled watching the remains of his home community go up in flames: "Already a ghost town by the end of 1943, Proctor was reduced to unsightly heaps of unwanted lumber and buildings that were to be burned. I recall standing on the graveyard hill in Possum Hollow and watching the Franklin store and warehouse being put to the torch by TVA"

TVA and the Park Service agreed to leave a few structures standing for park purposes. The Crate Hall cabin on Bone Valley Creek was preserved as a somewhat misleading example of the "pioneer existence" lived by the people in the area. Park Service officials also decided to leave the Calhoun house in Proctor and the Kress lodge at the junction of Bone Valley and Hazel Creek as ranger housing.

The residents of Hazel Creek left much more than unwanted lumber behind. As Duane Oliver recalled, "As they moved away from the creek, not everyone could take all of their furniture, and nearly every family left something behind that was later claimed by lumber 'scavengers,' burned with the buildings or left to rust." A number of cars and trucks which either could not be made to run or had no tires were also left behind. As former resident Henry Posey recalled to an *Asheville Citizen-Times* reporter in 1991, "We couldn't get any tires to bring them out on. It was wartime and there just were no tires. There were oodles of cars and trucks left on Hazel Creek. Most of them were cut up and buried by the Park Service." Some, however, were left intact and in place and provide a somewhat startling and ghostly reminder of the area's human history when unsuspecting hikers happen upon the rusting remains.

As the waters of the newly created Fontana Lake rose in late 1944, the final holdouts were forced to leave their homes behind. As resident Ray Shepherd re-

Duane Oliver

DUANE OLIVER, SHOWN HERE IN 1932, IS A NOTED LOCAL HISTORIAN WHO WROTE EXTENSIVELY ABOUT GROWING UP ON HAZEL CREEK AND THE HEARTBREAK OF LEAVING HIS ANCESTRAL HOME.

called, officials from T. V. A. told area residents, "We can take you out or you can swim out." Some waited to the last minute until "the critters were coming up from below. Because the water was coming up… you got raccoons and squirrels and snakes and deer… They said they had birds and squirrels and everything up in the rafters of the house. As that water was coming up that was the next safe haven so a lot of critters were coming up with that water." Appropriately, Granville Calhoun, now 69 years old, was reportedly the last person to move out.

Calhoun was able to arrange one last bear hunt that was recounted in a John Parris newspaper column. It does appear as if Calhoun misremembered the date—as he was entitled to do given the fact he was nearly 100 years old when the interview was conducted—of this hunt which was most likely in the fall of 1944, not 1946: "The last big hunt I was on was back in 1946. That was when the government took over all my property and I had to move out. But I reserved the right to hunt that fall and I invited all my friends for one last big bear hunt in the Smokies. The first day we run 16 bear and killed three. Reckon there was 50 to 75 shots fired that first day of the hunt. Next day we killed two bear, and before the season was over 27 had been killed on Hazel Creek."

By Christmas 1944, the families of Hazel Creek were scattered throughout western North Carolina and East Tennessee and celebrating the holiday in new homes and new churches. Duane Oliver asserts that given the small amount of industry in Swain County only about half stayed in the immediate area. Work at the Champion Fibre Company in Haywood County, the Enka Rayon Plant in Buncombe County, or Alcoa in Blount County, Tennessee attracted many to move further afield. Duane Oliver commented on the irony of Hazel Creek folks moving to East Tennessee, "reversing the migration that had brought their ancestors to the creek almost a century earlier."

That holiday, however, was a melancholy one for most former residents as they pondered what they had lost. Writer Florence Cope Bush in her classic account of life in the Great Smoky Mountains during the period, *Dorie: Woman of the Mountains*, effectively wraps up what this experience and its accompanying emotions must have been like for the Olivers, Calhouns, and others who were forced from their homes:

> The lumber companies had opened the door to the outside world. We became aware of "things"—things that money could buy, things that made life easier (or harder), things to see, things to do. They had opened a door—a door we were forced to use as an exit from our ancestral homes. Then, after the exit, the door was closed to us. We were given visitors' rights to the land—to come and look, but not to stay."

CHAPTER FIVE

Visitors' Rights

$\mathcal{S}$ince 1944, Hazel Creek has had no long-term human residents although interest in the area has followed the boom and bust pattern of the area's industrial era. The challenges of getting to Hazel Creek since the inundation of NC Highway 288 makes it a place where access requires determination and planning. One does not happen upon Hazel Creek. To get to the area requires either an 11.6 mile hike from Fontana Dam along the Lakeshore Trail; taking a boat shuttle five miles or so across Fontana Lake from Fontana Marina to the mouth of Hazel Creek (current cost, approximately $50 round trip); or, if you own or can rent a motorboat, canoe, or kayak, boating three miles across the lake from the U.S.D.A. Forest Service boat access ramp at Cable Cove.

For much of the time since 1944, primary interest in Hazel Creek has come from trout fisherman who make the pilgrimage to follow in the footsteps of Mark Cathey, Granville Calhoun, Jim Stikeleather, Jim Gasque, and others to tempt the large brown and rainbow trout with their dry flies and nymphs on Hazel, Bone Valley, and Walkers creek or take native speckled trout on their upper reaches. The marketing efforts of Stikeleather and Calhoun to attract clients to their hunting and fishing camps in the 1930s and early '40s helped spread the word about Hazel Creek's big trout and accessible fishing waters. Popular early hunting and fishing guides by Stikeleather's nephew Jim Gasque and by Samuel Hunnicutt, both of which went through multiple editions and were readily available into the 1960s, further burnished the watershed's reputation as world-class trout waters and as a bucket-list destination for any serious fly fisherman.

In later years, stories on Hazel Creek fishing regularly appeared in outdoor and fly fishing publications and its reputation and popularity only grew. In his 1985 work *Smoky Mountains Trout Fishing Guide*, Don Kirk asserted: "Hazel Creek has been termed 'the Crown Jewel' of trout fishing in the Great Smoky Mountains National Park and touted by most major outdoor publications in past years. Hazel Creek has all the needed qualifications to claim being the finest freestone stream in the Southern Appalachian Mountains." In 1991, Smokies fishing guide H. Lea Lawrence argued, "The creek deserves the accolades it has been given, because it is a beautiful and productive stream in an historic setting." Ian Rutter in his 2002 guide touts Hazel Creek as one of the few places anywhere where one can "catch a grand slam [in the eastern U.S. a brown, rainbow, and speckled trout caught in the same day] out of just one good run." Jim Casada adds that fishermen on Hazel Creek also have the potential for the even rarer Royal Slam; in addition to catching the three trout, landing a smallmouth bass or redeye in Hazel Creek's lower reaches.

Harry Middleton in his classic work *On the Spine of Time: A Flyfisher's Journey Among Mountains, People, Streams & Trout*, gave fishing on Hazel Creek an aura of mystery and magic that attracted even more attention from anglers and those seeking a spiritual experience in the backcountry. While Middleton's tales of a mystical and elusive bagpiper wandering the watershed and playing his eerie tunes or the strange backpacker who carried a Himalayan prayer wheel and claimed he was on a "mission to bring hope to these hard-luck mountains" were most likely metaphorical devices and probably did not actually happen, his work helped move a trip to Hazel Creek to the top of many an outdoor enthusiast's list with passages like:

> I come for the beauty and the good fishing rather than grand truths, though these too are here scattered about the creek bottoms like weathered stones. The soft light of dusk, a trout's rise, the sound of nothing but water over stones are glamour and excitement enough. Mountain solitude is deep and wide and abiding and yet coiled tight as a snake, something alive, ready to give way at any instant to something as ordinary as birdsong or as confounding and bewitching as a trout's sudden inexplicable leap out of a stream's cold waters and into the sun's bright warm light.

As remote as it is, local tourism promoters and creative fishermen helped to make Hazel Creek more accessible with a regular boat shuttle from Fontana Marina and with the invention of a strange contraption referred to either as a "Smoky Mountain pushcart" or, more commonly, as a "Hazel Creek buggie" or even "Hazel Creek Cadillac." These carts/buggies are generally made of light-weight tubular aluminum and bicycle wheels and "have the carrying capacity of half a dozen backpacks or more," according to author Jim Casada. The relatively flat and smooth

Hazel Creek Trail allows individuals "unwilling to compromise their fishing trips with the usual backcountry fare of freeze-dried foods and cramped hiking tents," to haul in, in Don Kirk's words, "Such backcountry rarities as coolers full of perishable foods, lanterns, cots, and big tents" as far as the Bone Valley backcountry site, 5.3 miles from the mouth of Hazel Creek. The time and inventor of the Hazel Creek buggie have been lost to the mists of time, but Casada remembers first seeing them in the 1970s and commonly seeing them in the 1980s.

The combination of improved accessibility, mystical aura, and, as Jim Casada observed, "too much positive press," has put pressure on the Hazel Creek fishery in recent years and caused some experts to downgrade the stream and its tributaries. In his 2009 Smokies flyfishing guide, Casada recalled growing up in the area and "one memorable trip after another to this storied stream.… Gradually though, the mystique and mesmerism vanished, victim of the angler's greatest enemy, too many fellow humans."

Despite the pressures of too many fishermen, drought in the late 2000s, and increasing fees for the shuttles, the most recent published guides still tout Hazel Creek as a fishing destination. Guide Steve Claxton observed in 2011 that negative press and the increase in transportation costs have kept anglers away and "the fishing pressure seems to have decreased a bit." Casada eloquently wrapped up his viewpoint, that despite the human pressure:

> Still, Hazel Creek has remained resilient, and there are probably as many trout as ever. It's just that they draw far more attention than once was the case and as a result my visits to this one-time stream of dreams have been considerably curtailed. Having said that though, the pilgrimage to Hazel Creek is one every serious Smokies fisherman should make at least once. Then you can decide whether a return trip is your angling cup of tea.

In the early 1980s, interest in the Hazel Creek area temporarily shifted to the sizable inholdings on nearby Eagle Creek, the site of the old Fontana Copper Mine, and on Sugar Fork at the old Adams mine. TVA had been unable to come to an agreement with the North Carolina Exploration Company (part of the Cities Services Corporation) over three tracts of land totaling 2,343.7 acres the company owned when the federal government initially purchased land on the north shore of the Little Tennessee River in the 1940s. The mines had ceased operations when the waters of Fontana Lake inundated NC Highway 288 in 1944, but until the 1980s, despite the fact that no mining had taken place for years, Cities Services and the National Park Service were unable to come to an agreement on a fair purchase price and the NPS was loathe to haul a corporation with such deep pockets into court in a condemnation procedure.

Over the years, however, the abandoned inholdings began to pose problems for park managers. The relatively unsupervised properties served as convenient staging grounds for poachers seeking bear, wild hogs, or ginseng. As park spokesperson

Roger Miller commented in 1983, "Hunting on the property formerly owned by Cities Service Corp. and poaching on neighboring park lands have been a constant threat to endangered plant and animal species." In 1983, the Park Service and Cities Services came to an agreement and the federal government purchased the land for inclusion in Great Smoky Mountains National Park for a little less than $1 million.

Local stories floating around the Swain County area often assert that in eliminating the possibility of re-opening mining operations on Cities Services property with its alleged rich copper, gold, and silver deposits, the Park service deprived the county of millions of dollars in tax revenue and hundreds of well-paying jobs. However, mining surveys done by MIT geologist E. H. Emmons in 1942 and '43 and by Robert O'Brien, mining engineer for the National Park Service, in 1972 concluded that mining the Fontana mine would be a money-losing proposition. O'Brien asserted in his report that the costs "necessary to re-equip the mine, build the mill and mine out the existing ore body" would be $3,630,000 "for equipment and facilities as well as working capital." Given the estimated value of the ore still in the ground, "the operation would be a losing proposition. The only condition which could make this a marginally profitable operation would be an ore body at least 4 times as large as the present ore body." While some may argue that Emmons and O'Brien were part of a government conspiracy to low-ball Cities Services and shut down a lucrative mine, the simple facts that in 40 years the company did not try to re-open the mines and that it sold the property for a relatively low price further indicate that the ore in the Hazel Creek/Eagle Creek area has little commercial value.

The lingering issue that has brought Hazel Creek the most public attention after 1944, especially since the early 1970s, has been the 1943 promise by the federal government to replace NC Highway 288 and the creation of the so-called "Road to Nowhere." The controversy centers on the four-party agreement signed July 30, 1943 between TVA, the Department of the Interior, the State of North Carolina, and Swain County. In that agreement, the State agreed to build a road connecting U.S. Highway 19 in Bryson City to the eastern border of Great Smoky Mountains National Park and the Department of the Interior agreed, "as soon as funds are made available for that purpose by Congress after the cessation of the hostilities in which the United States is now engaged [World War II]," to "construct or cause to be constructed" a road "hereinafter collectively referred to as the 'Park Road.'" Park officials planned the road so it would connect Fontana Dam to the new state road just north of Bryson City. In addition, T. V. A. placed $400,000 in trust with the State for Swain County to cover the bond debt the county had incurred to construct NC Highway 288.

In 1943, local leaders and managers for Great Smoky Mountains National Park hailed the agreement as both a boon for the Swain County economy and as an integral part of the Park Service's plan to bring tourists to the newly dedicated park. A 1943 editorial in the *Bryson City Times* asserted, "Anyone with the smallest amount of imagination can visualize what a road of this kind will mean to Bryson City… There is nothing that can keep Bryson City from becoming the tourist center of Eastern America." For the National Park Service, the so-called "Park Road" was part of the GSMNP master plan for an "'around the Park road' of which the Park section of a project road between Deals Gap and Bryson City constitutes an important link."

Given the exigencies of war time and the understandable need for post-war recovery, most of the parties involved knew that neither the State of North Carolina nor the Park Service would complete these projects overnight, especially given the fact that they depended on appropriations from both the North Carolina General Assembly and the U.S. Congress. Work on a one-mile link over Fontana Dam to the park border did begin in 1947 and was completed the next year at a cost of $400,000. In 1949, the Park Service constructed a one-lane, dirt access road from Fontana Dam to a few cemeteries.

By the late 1940s, however, frustration over the slow pace of the project began to boil over. In 1949, Bryson City attorney T. D. Bryson and U.S. Representative Monroe Redden of Hendersonville and North Carolina's 12th Congressional District issued a demand that the federal government either build the road or return the land on the north shore of Fontana Lake to Swain County. Redden followed up with a bill requiring Congress to return the land to the county, as "Congress will perhaps never appropriate that much money [costs were estimated at the time at $10 million] for this purpose; certainly not in the foreseeable future will this be done." The bill died in committee.

Swain Countians did see some progress in the 1950s on the fulfillment of the promised roads especially from the State of North Carolina. In 1958, the State completed the three-mile link between Bryson City and the eastern border of the park. In addition, the North Carolina State Highway Commission improved and paved a number of existing roads in Swain and neighboring Graham County and connected Bryson City to Fontana Dam by way of U.S. Highway 19 and NC Highway 28. For some Park Service officials and for growing numbers of environmentalists, the construction of NC Highway 28—referred to by some as the "South Shore Road"—fulfilled the spirit of the 1943 agreement by connecting Bryson City, Fontana Dam, and Deals Gap making the reconstruction of NC Highway 288—now often referred to as the "North Shore Road"—unnecessary. Indeed, concerns about both the expense and environmental damage of constructing the road began to surface as early as 1950. A National Park Service report that year noted, "The entire route lies in extremely difficult country so badly cut up by ravines and sharp ridges that it is not possible to follow the contour closely with a standard location. The result is a location of heavy cuts and fills requiring large expenditures for grading, drainage structures and roadside development."

Map of Hazel Creek Area

THIS MAP SHOWS THE RUGGED TERRAIN ON THE NORTH SHORE OF FONTANA
LAKE ALONG THE ROUTE OF THE PROPOSED REPLACEMENT FOR NC
HIGHWAY 288.

As the 1960s rolled around, opposition to the road within the Park Service and among environmentalists began to grow due to both the estimated high costs and concerns over the environmental impact of road construction. In an internal memo, Park Service official William Zimmer asserted, "the proposed Bryson City-Fontana Road is an unjustifiable extravagance, notwithstanding the iron-bound three-way [actually four-way] agreement." Environmentalist Henry Wilson called the "iron-bound agreement" anachronistic in a letter to Secretary of the Interior Stewart Udall in 1962: "I am all for the sanctity of contract but if many years ago the government agreed to maintain a cavalry troop in Bryson City to defend against Indian attacks, would it still feel compelled to do so?"

At the same time, political pressures to build the road mounted. In a scathing 1960 letter to Secretary of the Interior Fred Seaton, North Carolina Governor Luther Hodges lambasted the federal government for failure to build the road in a timely fashion: "I express the firm view that the Department of the Interior has an obligation to give more than lip service to the fulfillment of its contractual agreement." Hodges also responded to the concern of environmentalists that road construction would "despoil a virgin or primeval wilderness" pointing out that until 1944, significant numbers of people populated the area. He also challenged the contention that the South Shore Road (NC 28) provided a suitable alternative to the proposed North

Shore Road asserting that NC 28 "was not constructed nor intended to serve as a major traffic route nor as a substitute for the anticipated north shore road."

As for the concerns of environmentalists, road supporters responded that Hazel Creek and the North Shore area were anything but pristine wilderness. In a 1960 *Asheville Citizen* article, Granville Calhoun opined:

> Untouched wilderness? Why it's a joke. It's been picked clean. By the time the virgin stuff was gone they started on the second growth. I have a feeling that most of those who oppose the road don't know pea-turkey about Hazel Creek except what they've read in wildlife magazines and newspaper columns by writers who've got an ax to grind and want folks to believe something that just isn't true.

> Man's mark is still upon the land. Anybody with eyesight that travels about Hazel Creek can see the signs of it. Why there's a dozen graveyards. If it's wilderness that's never been touched by man, how do they account for them? Or the railroad beds that scar the hillsides? Or the steel bridge built across the creek 50 years ago? And what about the old car wrecks along the creek and the rusting wheels off the railroad cars?

Calhoun concluded by asserting that the road, "wouldn't hit a virgin tree anywhere."

Citizen-Times columnist John Parris echoed Calhoun's arguments and talked about an issue that became increasingly important to road supporters, access to cemeteries in the area:

> In the Hazel Creek-Forney-Eagle Creek area there are at least 16 cemeteries, many of them—especially those on Hazel Creek—that are practically inaccessible. But if the Bryson City—Fontana road is ever built, then those folks whose kin lie buried in these far-off, out-of-the-way graveyards can get to them and clean them of weeds and briars and sprouts and repair the gravestones that have been tumbled and carried off by the bear. All of which goes to show that the idea that Hazel Creek nestles in a primeval state is ridiculous.

Parris even challenged Hazel Creek's vaunted reputation as a world-class trout stream. "For the Hazel Creek of fact, fiction and fancy not only is an abandoned settlement but is also the most overrated trout stream in the mountains."

In response to the pressure, the National Park Service finally began construction of the North Shore Road in 1960. That year they awarded a contract for a 2.3-mile section of road from the eastern park boundary to Canebrake Branch.

Even as the Park Service continued work on the road, however, Park Service officials proposed a new idea. As part of the its "Mission 66" plan—a ten-year program to make the national parks more "user friendly" by improving existing roads, constructing new ones, and upgrading and constructing new visitor facilities—Park Superintendent George Fry offered an alternative to the North Shore Road. Instead, the Park Service would build a 34.7-mile transmountain highway inside the park that would rise from Monteith Branch, climb the upper reaches of Hazel Creek, cross the divide at Buckeye Gap, and descend Miry Ridge, connecting Bryson City with Townsend, Tennessee. In negotiations with Swain County officials in 1964, Fry secured an agreement to substitute the new transmountain road for the North Shore Road specified in the 1943 agreement. The people of Swain County rejoiced at the prospect of becoming a major park entrance and many residents believed that they would finally reap their fair share of tourist traffic and revenue.

The proposed project sparked an enthusiastic response from federal officials, politicians, and civic leaders. Director of the National Park Service and former Assistant Superintendent of Great Smoky Mountains National Park, George Hartzog, threw his support behind the project and defended the building of the road through an area many considered wilderness. "You can't just order a visitor to get out of his car," he argued "you have to entice him out of his car. We may be able to show, through motor-nature trails, short nature walks, lookouts, outdoor exhibits, or other methods of interpretation the meaning of wilderness and what it can offer." Western North Carolina U.S. Congressman Roy Taylor argued, "There is room for abundant wilderness areas and, at the same time, room for another highway to make the park more accessible and enjoyable." North Carolina Governor Dan K. Moore added: "The National Park Service, in fulfilling its legal and moral obligations, to construct this road is doing something about dispersing traffic which is now cluttering the highways, and the proposed road would be the least damaging to conservationists." Governor Frank Clement of Tennessee and Knoxville U.S. Representative John Duncan also supported the transmountain road and voiced their support in public hearings. Civic and regional booster groups also chimed in. Carlos Campbell, a Knoxville leader in the original park movement and the author of a history of the park's establishment, argued strongly for the road: "Any person who asks that neither road be built clearly indicates, it seems to me, that such a person is either grossly ignorant of the historic background of the controversy or he is asking the Park Service to violate a valid contract, thus asking it to take a position of sheer dishonesty." The three major newspapers in the region—the *Asheville Citizen;* the *Knoxville Sentinel;* and the *Knoxville News*—also endorsed the plan.

However, road boosters had greatly underestimated the strength of the growing environmental movement. New organizations committed to environmental and wilderness protection cropped up every day in the wake of the publication of Rachel Carson's *Silent Spring* and the passage of the Wilderness Act in 1964. Knoxville

George Fry

SUPERINTENDENT FRY PROPOSED AN ALTERNATE PLAN TO THE NORTH
SHORE ROAD, A TRANSMOUNTAIN ROAD THAT WOULD CROSS THE
CREST OF THE SMOKIES AND CONNECT BRYSON CITY TO TOWNSEND,
TENNESSEE. ALTHOUGH ENTHUSIASTICALLY SUPPORTED BY POLI-
TICIANS AND BUSINESS LEADERS, OPPOSITION FROM THE GROWING
ENVIRONMENTAL MOVEMENT DOOMED IT.

lawyer Harvey Broome, one of the founders and later President of the Wilderness
Society, led the fight against the road. His good friend and fellow member of the
Smoky Mountains Hiking Club, Ernie Dickerman joined him. Dickerman argued,
"You can't build a road through the wilderness and still have a wilderness—the two
things are incompatible."

The Wilderness Society issued an S.O.S.—"Save Our Smokies"—to its 35,000
members and to the nation-at-large. It called on people who cared about wilderness
to either attend one of the two hearings on the road or to register their opposition

Carlos Campbell

CARLOS CAMPBELL, A KNOXVILLE COMMUNITY LEADER AND AUTHOR, AND EARLY SUPPORTER OF THE PARK, ALSO ENDORSED FRY'S PLAN.

to Superintendent Fry. At a public hearing in Gatlinburg on June 13, 1966, the Wilderness Society, Trout Unlimited, the Smoky Mountains Hiking Club, the Izaak Walton League, the National Parks Association, the Wildlife Federation, the Appalachian Trail Club, the Sierra Club, and Supreme Court Justice William O. Douglas all voiced their disfavor. Dickerman also generated a substantial show of opposition two days later at a hearing in the heart of the enemy camp, Bryson City. Representatives from the Carolina Mountain Club, Carolina Bird Club, the Georgia Appalachian Trail Club, Defenders of Wildlife, and several area college professors expressed their belief that the road was a bad idea. Dr. Dan Hale—a NASA physicist from Huntsville, Alabama—called the transmountain road a "colossal boondoggle" and delineated the reasons he believed Swain County had already been compensated for their lost road. A college student who had traveled from Rochester, New York reminded the crowd that Great Smoky Mountains National Park "did not belong to North Carolinians or Tennesseans but rather to all Americans." He cautioned that "the tourist dollar should not override the interests of a majority of Americans." *The New York Time*s even chimed in with an editorial arguing, "Slashing and tunneling through the last mountain wilderness in the East is a destructive solution to a local economic problem."

Road supporters attempted to counter the arguments of environmentalists. An editorial in the *Asheville Citizen* ridiculed their concerns. "Certainly if civilization is to salvage anything of value from its headlong extravagance, it ought to save a few places where man can go to contemplate his idiocy. But preservation for the mere sake of isolation—preservation as an idealistic concept—amounts to indulging a pointless whim." While many Swain Countians dismissed road opponents as "wilderness creeps," Velma Benton offered a more plaintive response in the "Backtalk" section of the *Citizen*. "It would be a shame if the government said 'Forget about it [the commitment to build the road], it is only a contract.' Me, I am just a widow with a 14-year-old daughter, but I have a contract with the government as my daughter and I get Social Security. I feel if the government could just up and break one contract they could break any contract." Park Superintendent Fry argued that the area of concern was not a "true wilderness" as it had been "logged over and burned over." He further asserted that environmentalists should not be concerned as the road "would largely follow natural contours and traverse the park in such a way as to avoid undue damage to superlative park values."

However, opponents of the road found a sympathetic ear in the Secretary of the Interior Stewart Udall. The year before he entered office Udall declared, "[t]he one overriding principle of the conservation movement is that no work of man (save the bare minimum of roads, trails, and necessary public facilities in access areas) should intrude into the wonder places of the National Park System." In the Buckeye Gap area of the park, site of the proposed road, Harvey Broome discovered and documented such a wonder place, the southernmost stands of red spruce in North America. Armed with this information, Broome and Dickerman energized the local community and wilderness proponents nationwide to voice their opposition in a protest hike. On October 23, 1966, 576 individuals, including the 81-year-old Reverend Rufus Morgan, signed in at Clingmans Dome to participate in a "Save-Our-Smokies" hike. Much to the dismay of Swain County residents—and many in Blount County, Tennessee—Secretary Udall announced on December 10, 1967, that he would not approve construction of the transmountain road.

Despite this setback, the "iron-clad agreement" to replace NC Highway 288 still stood, and construction of the road continued, albeit slowly. By 1970, the Park Service had built six miles of road culminating in a 1,200-foot tunnel. In 1971, however, the Park Service ceased all construction on the road amid mounting environmental and fiscal concerns. Environmental concerns centered on the potential exposure by road construction of acidic Anakeesta rock found in the North Shore area. Officials feared that exposure of this rock would leach acid and heavy metals into area streams killing aquatic life. In addition, they expressed concern about the negative impact on wildlife, particularly bears whose habitat would be divided and reduced by the road. The expense of building such a road also became increasingly prohibitive, especially as Congressional appropriations for the Park Service began a long period of decline.

However, the road issue was not about to die and in the mid-1970s local supporters of the road began to organize effectively to see the contract honored. Most of the organizing sprang from the first of what became annual Hazel Creek Reunions held at the Deep Creek Picnic Area near Bryson City in July 1976. To the surprise of organizers, over 400 people showed up. Duane Oliver observed that three topics dominated the conversations of the reunion attendees: the completion of the North Shore Road—now popularly termed the "Road to Nowhere"—the disrepair of many of the cemeteries on the North Shore, particularly the ones on Hazel Creek and its tributaries, and the lack of attention and often imperious attitude toward locals and their concerns on the part of officials at Great Smoky Mountains National Park.

The attitude within the National Park Service that locals should leave decision making in the parks to the "experts" was, unfortunately, one that came to permeate the system through the 1950s, '60s, and '70s making interactions between park officials and local groups tense at best. In places like Swain County, where memories of removal and unaddressed issues simmered not far below the surface, relationships often proved downright hostile. As former backcountry ranger Duncan Hollar, who worked the North Shore for several years observed, "The Park Service had no dealings with the local people whatsoever at the time… The Park was an island and did whatever it wanted, and there was no interaction with the local community."

This lack of communication came to a head in the mid-1970s over the issue of cemeteries and their maintenance during the short tenure of Smokies Superintendent Boyd Evison. While many remember Evison for several positive innovations in the Park, he often butted heads with locals. Evison first angered former residents of the Park when he announced that plastic flowers would no longer be allowed as grave decorations and directed maintenance personal to remove flowers that were not bio-degradable. This actually brought increased focus on cemeteries and the Park Service maintenance supervisor on the North Shore came under fire for being, in the words of Claude Douthit, "very lax" in his attention to cemetery maintenance. Indeed, attendees at the first Hazel Creek reunion lamented the fact that no grave decorations had taken place in many of the watershed's cemeteries since 1944 and

Harvey Broome

KNOXVILLE LAWYER AND PRESIDENT OF THE WILDERNESS SOCIETY, HARVEY BROOME, LED THE OPPOSITION TO THE TRANSMOUNTAIN ROAD AND HELPED ORGANIZE THE "SAVE OUR SMOKIES" HIKE.

that a number of the cemeteries had fallen into disrepair.

After that first Hazel Creek Reunion in 1976, cemetery care and maintenance became a focal issue for both the revival of the memory of Hazel Creek and other North Shore communities and the revival of the road issue. The Proctor Cemetery was the only Hazel Creek cemetery that had received routine maintenance as descendants of many of the early families in the Proctor area, organized by Ferman Farley and Jack Cable, had regularly cleaned and decorated the cemetery since 1945. Others in the area, in the words of Duane Oliver, "were in a ruinous state." In 1977, Helen Cable Vance and Mildred Cable Johnson organized the North Shore Cemetery Association (NSCA) and the North Shore Historical Association (NSHA). One of the primary goals of the Cemetery Association was to remedy this situation, but getting people to these remote places was a daunting task.

Whether from a sense of doing the right thing or in an attempt to head off the revival of the North Shore Road issue, officials at the Great Smoky Mountains National Park began to cooperate with the NSCA to better maintain the cemeteries and provide access for annual decorations. In 1978, former North Shore residents and their families held Decoration Days for the first time since the mid 1940s at the Cable, Bone Valley, and Hall Cemeteries. The Park Service, along with private individuals using their own boats, provided transportation across the lake. Participants reached their cemeteries, in the words of Duane Oliver, "on foot, horse-drawn wagons and motorized transport." The Park Service continues to provide transportation to family members for cemetery decorations to the present day.

Cemetery care was not the only important issue to the NSCA and it soon became the center of local activism in support of road construction. In the 1980s the organization and individual members took significant actions to push the process forward. In 1983, Helen Vance and 25 others filed suit in federal court to force the National Park Service to provide road access to the cemeteries. While the judge ruled that the 26 plaintiffs did not have standing to file suit as they "were not a party to the original [1943] agreement," the court action put Park Service officials on notice that the issue was far from dead.

In 1986, acting Superintendent David Mihalic stirred up a hornet's nest among road proponents when he proposed removing two steel truss bridges spanning Hazel Creek built during the Ritter era. Fearing loss of access to cemeteries and sensing a campaign by the Park Service to remove all vestiges of human activity in the area and designate the area as federally protected "wilderness"—which would kill any chance of the road being built—the move drew vehement protests from the NSCA and NSHA as a "slap in the face to the people who once lived…" in the area. The move led some road proponents to compare the treatment of the former residents of Hazel Creek and their descendants to victims of the Trail of Tears and the Holocaust. Ruth Chandler wrote an article in *Fontana*, the newsletter of NSHA, protesting the undue attention she believed outside wilderness advocates received from the Park Service and the lack of attention paid to the views of those who had lived in the area and their descendants. "We are a God-fearing, peace-loving people. Why do we suffer because a few stranger[s], to us and our area, can dictate what our government can or cannot do?" In July 1986, 53 individuals, organized by NSCA, walked three-and-a-half miles along the road grade of NC Highway 288 to protest and challenge the removal of the bridges.

In the aftermath of the bridge controversy, road proponents gained an important and powerful ally when North Carolina U.S. Senator Jesse Helms took up the cause. While he had received the nickname "Senator No" from the press due to his consistent opposition to federal spending, Helms found in the fulfillment of the 1943 promise an expenditure of federal tax dollars to which he could give an enthusiastic "Yes." In March 1987, Helms introduced a bill to appropriate $950,000 to construct a "primitive road to provide access to the cemeteries north of Fontana Lake," pay Swain County $9.5 million in cash, forgive the debt on a Farmer's Home Administration loan the county had taken out to build a new high school, and absolve the federal

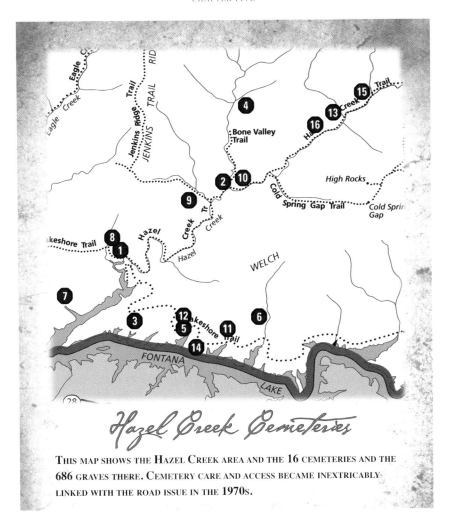

Hazel Creek Cemeteries

THIS MAP SHOWS THE HAZEL CREEK AREA AND THE 16 CEMETERIES AND THE 686 GRAVES THERE. CEMETERY CARE AND ACCESS BECAME INEXTRICABLY LINKED WITH THE ROAD ISSUE IN THE 1970S.

government of its responsibility to replace NC Highway 288. Helms asserted: "I offer this bill to assure justice to the people who entered into an agreement with their federal government in 1943 and to redeem the honor and integrity of the federal government." While Helms' bill died in committee, he would continue to serve as a strong advocate for the road throughout his long Senate career.

Action in the Senate by another U.S. Senator to address the road issue made the situation in Swain County increasingly tense and confrontational. Tennessee U.S. Senator Jim Sasser came up with a proposal to settle the road issue and permanently designate the North Shore area as federally protected wilderness. In August 1987, Sasser made a fact-finding trip with National Park Service officials to actually see the Road to Nowhere. Road supporters got wind of the Sasser visit and 30 gathered to protest the plan and confront Sasser. Two of the protesters, according to the *Asheville Citizen-Times*, "briefly blocked passage through a tunnel." Marvin Grant, one of the protesters "was physically removed by park rangers." Linda Hogue confronted Sasser: "You owe us the courtesy of talking to us. We don't want this wilderness." Sasser did not help matters when he spouted back, "I have heard your stories and you have had your say... I'm not going to listen to everybody in Swain County."

Despite the protests, Sasser introduced his bill into the Senate calling for wilderness designation and a $9.5 million payout to Swain County to settle the road agreement. The Sasser bill prompted an impassioned plea in *Fontana* for justice from road supporter Rev. George Britt:

> While a maniacal greed and a frenzied pursuit of sensuality have gripped this nation until it has lost all sense of its destiny and leads the world in murders, robberies, pornography, crimes in the streets and in high places, here on the periphery of the land that was their former home is an endangered species, the salt of America, a little reservoir of the sturdy, honest, pious, moral, patriotic stock which made the greatness of the America of the eighteenth and nineteenth centuries. To them it is very much like a religious pilgrimage to have access to return to their sacred home sites and cemeteries and reminisce about the America that used to be.
>
> I hope in this year of celebrating the two hundredth anniversary of our Constitution, which guarantees 'liberty and justice for all,' this injustice can be rectified.

While the Sasser bill made it through a Senate subcommittee, Sen. Helms killed it before it reached the floor of the Senate.

In the following months, the road issue became an increasingly partisan political football. Democrats generally favored wilderness designation and some sort of pay out to Swain County and Republicans generally favored building at least a primitive road. Helms gained an ally in his efforts in 1990 when western North Carolina voters elected Brevard Republican Charles Taylor to the U.S. House of Representatives. Taylor, dubbed "Chainsaw Charlie" by environmentalists due to his extensive timber holdings in western North Carolina and his opposition to environmental protection legislation, was elected for eight consecutive terms and soon became the North Shore Road's chief advocate in the U.S. Congress.

Helms and Taylor's support encouraged "build the road" proponents in Swain County. In response to the Sasser bill, locals had formed a new organization, Citizens Against Wilderness, with local school teacher Linda Hogue as its president. In 1992, Hogue wrote an editorial for the A*sheville Citizen-Times* where she touted not only the need to honor the 1943 promise and provide access to cemeteries, but revived arguments on the potential economic benefits the road would bring: "Asking Swain County, 'Do you want the road or the money?' is like asking, 'Do you want the goose or the golden egg?'" She continued blaming "radical environmentalists"

Jesse Helms

ONE OF THE FEW FEDERAL PROJECTS THAT NORTH
CAROLINA'S "SENATOR NO" FAVORED WAS
CONSTRUCTION OF THE NORTH SHORE ROAD. HE
BECAME THE ROAD'S STRONGEST CONGRESSIONAL
PROPONENT UP UNTIL HIS RETIREMENT FROM THE
SENATE IN 2003.

who "began screaming propaganda" for killing the road. Other road proponents echoed Hogue's criticism of outside environmentalists and accused the Park Service of intentionally dragging its feet until everyone who cared about the road issue died off. Larry Vickery asserted the Park Service had "just been pushing us back, postponing all this until ninety-nine and forty-four hundredths percent of us are dead, and they'd say, 'Well, it don't matter anymore.' And once we quit visiting the cemeteries, they'll go back to nature, which is what the Park Service wants. It's what the environmentalist wackos want, you know. They don't want anybody over there except themselves. They don't care if some old person wants to go over there and visit the grave of her father or grandfather. They don't care."

Legislation of some sort related to the road came up in Congress almost every other year in the late '80s, through the '90s, and into the 2000s. In 1991, North Carolina U.S. Senator Terry Sanford introduced a bill for wilderness designation and a $16 million payout. Helms introduced bills in 1991, '93, '95, and '96 calling for construction of a primitive road plus a $16 million payout. All were short-lived and failed to make it out of committee. However, in 2000, Helms and Taylor used their seniority and influence to slip through a $16 million appropriation in a transportation bill to fund an environmental impact study (EIS) to research the possible impact of road construction.

As road supporters dug in their heels in the aftermath of the successful Helms/ Taylor legislation, however, by the early 2000s support for road construction, even in Swain County, began to wane. In 2002, a group of Swain County residents formed a pro-settlement group called Citizens for the Economic Future of Swain County. A brochure published by the group argued, "For 59 years we have heard, 'A deal is a deal, a promise is a promise, an eye for an eye, a road for a road.' Yes, it's wrong for the government to treat us this way, but it is time for us to make the best of a bad situation." Duane Oliver even came out in favor of a settlement: "I strongly support a financial settlement that would possibly provide for a Swain County historical museum, a section of which would honor the lost communities of the North Shore area. The county will never be able to afford a decent museum, good roads or schools, or anything else it needs from the construction of the North Shore road, if it's ever built at all." For the first time in 2002, the voters of Swain County elected a publicly pro-settlement majority to its county commission and in 2003, the Commission voted 4 - 1, with road supporter David Monteith casting the only "no" vote, to support a resolution calling for a settlement of $52 million.

Even as many Swain Countians became convinced that the road would never be built and that the best the county could do was to secure a cash settlement, the process to study the feasibility of building the road mandated by the Helms/Taylor bill moved forward. In 2002, the Federal Highway Administration hired a firm to conduct the required EIS and in 2003, the National Park Service began "scoping meetings" in the region to assess public views on the issue. Some of the meetings reflected the intense feelings on both sides of the issue. At a March 2003 meeting at Swain County High School, Linda Hogue reportedly told two University of Tennessee students who were handing out Sierra Club stickers, "We'd just as soon the Sierra Club stayed out of our business."

In January 2006, the National Park Service released a 522-page preliminary EIS on the road. It listed five possible actions that the Park Service would consider:

1. No action.
2. A $52 million cash settlement to Swain County.
3. Construction of a picnic area at Laurel Branch at a cost of $13.7 million.
4. Construction of part of the road to Bushnell at a cost of $148.6 million.
5. Construction of the full North Shore Road at a cost of $600 million.

The Park Service solicited input and comments on the EIS and over the next three months received over 70,000 letters, emails, and faxes.

Following the Park Service report, the *Asheville Citizen-Times* editorial board offered their views in an article weighing the issues and calling on Swain County to accept a settlement:

> There are several things that shouldn't be overlooked.
>
> There are feelings of the wronged parties in this affair from the isolated communities. Blame who you will, the fact is they were treated shabbily. If their concerns are casually pushed aside because of very legitimate worries over loss of bear habitat or damage to species, it ignores their dignity and is probably the best way to create anti-environmentalists. They've been cut off from something they love.
>
> But communities like Hazel Creek are gone. A road isn't going to bring them back. In fact, there's a good argument to be made that a road built with the good intention of providing access to cemeteries is going to become just another entry route to herds of outsiders bent on leaf-looking, hiking or tooling around tight curves, pretty much everything but taking an interest in the culture and people who once lived in the area. In that sense there's a chance what's left of places like Proctor and Hazel Creek will vanish even faster.
>
> We have to honor the past without compromising the future. While we sympathize with the displaced families, with a soaring national deficit, the cost of completing the road simply can't be justified, especially in light of the environmental damage it could cause.

Later in 2006, the road issue became part of one of the more intense political battles in western North Carolina history, the contest for the area's seat in the U.S. Congress. Many observers firmly believed that after eight consecutive terms Charles Taylor had a lock on the office. Those observers, however, did not count on the emergence of perhaps the one Democrat who could defeat Taylor in the conservative-leaning district. Born and raised in Swain County, Heath Shuler became a *Parade Magazine* All-American quarterback at Swain County High, runner-up for the Heisman Trophy at the University of Tennessee, a first-round draft pick for the Washington Redskins, and now owned a highly successful real estate business. Shuler was also the kind of Democrat who could win in the region, a so-called "Blue Dog," evangelical Christian, pro-gun, and anti-abortion.

Shuler also had a very close personal connection to the Road to Nowhere and differed with Taylor on the issue. Shuler argued that the road was "a political issue for Taylor but a personal issue for him." Growing up, he often went to an overlook on the road to make important decisions, including his decision to sign a scholarship offer with the University of Tennessee, and even proposed to his wife at that same overlook. He called for a cash settlement and defended his decision by asserting, "I totally 100 percent respect their [road supporters] viewpoint because it is home to so many of these people. But I also respect that God gave us some incredible gifts, and our environment is certainly one of them, and we must protect it the best way we possibly can."

Taylor countered Shuler's arguments by asserting that the EIS was not accurate, that a good road could be built more cheaply than the Park Service estimate, and that it would not cause much environmental damage. "I am firmly convinced the road can be built more cheaply and with no more environmental damage than was done by building the road into Cades Cove [on the Tennessee side of the Smokies]." He called for construction of the full road, a museum to commemorate local history and culture and honor those removed from the area, and a cash settlement for Swain and Graham counties.

With Shuler's defeat of Taylor in the November 2006 election, however, it appeared inevitable that the issue would be finally resolved with a cash settlement. Since Helms had retired from the Senate in 2003 and with Taylor now out of office, no champion of the road remained on the federal level. As D. J. Gerken of the Southern Environmental Law Center observed, "It's just a fact that Charles Taylor was the force in Washington pushing for this road, the only force." On October 2, 2007, the National Park Service and the Federal Highway Administration released its final EIS recommending "a financial settlement to Swain County in lieu of building the road, sometimes called the 'Road to Nowhere.'" The report cited the "major, adverse, long-term impacts to topography, geology, and soils," as a deciding factor.

It took almost two-and-a-half years for federal and Swain County officials to hash out an agreement and reach a final settlement, but on February 6, 2010, representatives for Swain County and the federal government gathered at Swain County High School to sign the papers to settle the road issue once and for all with a $52 million payout. Secretary of the Interior Ken Salazar was scheduled to attend the ceremony, but a blizzard in the Mid-Atlantic states prevented him from leaving D.C. Salazar therefore signed in D.C. and a staffer conveyed the document to North Carolina and Swain County Commission chair Glenn Jones signed on behalf of the county with Smokies Superintendent Dale Ditmanson standing by.

The federal government structured the payout so that Swain County received a $12.8 million initial payment, with an immediate $4 million payment and an additional $8.8 million coming within 120 days. Congress was to appropriate the final $39.2 million in incremental payments over the next ten years. The federal government paid the initial funds into an account managed by the North Carolina State Treasurer and Swain County receives annual payouts from the fund based on interest return. The county is only allowed to tap the principal on the fund if two-thirds of the voters of Swain County approve such a withdrawal. At a six percent return, the initial down-payment on the fund would yield $768,000 in revenue to the perennially cash-strapped county where 85% of the land is owned by the federal government under management of TVA, the National Park Service, the U.S.D.A. Forest Service, and the Eastern Band of the Cherokee. With the full payout on deposit and at the same rate, Swain County could plan on $3 million in additional revenue per year, a sizable amount for a county with an average annual budget of around $10 million.

Supporters hailed the landmark agreement with many crediting Congressman Shuler as the catalyst for finally settling the contentious issue. Superintendent Ditmanson asserted, "I cannot emphasize enough that the resolution of the monetary settlement would still be at an impasse without the personal commitment of Heath Shuler and his staff." Gary Wade, Chairman emeritus for Friends of the Smokies, argued, "As a native of Swain County, only Shuler could have led the successful effort to resolve this long standing dispute." Shuler himself praised the agreement which he claimed would "bring much-needed resources to Swain County for decades to come." While he was not as enthusiastic as the others, County Commissioner Steve Moon, a long-time proponent of the cash settlement, wearily noted, "We need closure, we need to move on. To me, it's the only thing that makes sense. They are not going to build the road."

Road supporters, however, expressed their extreme displeasure with the signing. David Monteith, the only Swain County Commissioner to vote against the settlement, had led a campaign to hold public meetings and a referendum on the issue and defiantly asserted, "I'd rather work for this road for another 67 years before I sell away the heritage of our children to a bunch of crazy environmentalists." Vivian Cook, a Bryson City road supporter, expressed her disappointment with Congressman Shuler, "Shuler has been a big let-down for native people of the North Shore who gave up a good life when forced from their homes and businesses only to be lied to by our government." Somewhat resigned to the inevitability of the settlement, Monteith did hope that some of the money generated by the fund would be used for a museum to honor the memory of the people removed from Hazel Creek and other North Shore communities: "That would be a tribute to the people that gave everything."

While settlement supporters hailed the agreement for finally settling the issue, the subsequent efforts to get Congress to appropriate even part of the final $39.2 million payout to Swain County have yielded little fruit and continue to frustrate both road supporters and road opponents. Despite the fact that President Barack Obama appropriated $4 million for the settlement in the Park Service budget in 2012, officials will not release the money without direct authorization from Congress. Bills introduced by Shuler's successor, Republican Mark Meadows, in 2013 and by Senator Kay Hagan, a Democrat, in 2014 to provide that authorization never made it out of committee. The money promised to Swain County has become the victim of a dysfunctional Congress and of what an editorialist for the *Asheville Citizen-Times* termed "earmarks theater." While the payout is part of a contracted obligation of the federal government, it has erroneously become tagged by Congressional budget hawks as an earmark, designed to benefit a small group at the expense of the entire country.

Swain County has reaped some benefit from the $12.8 million downpayment on the settlement. Most visibly, the county has been able to renovate its 1909 courthouse complete with a visitors' center run by the Swain County Chamber of Commerce and a store run by the Great Smoky Mountains Association featuring park-related merchandise and publications. The best part of the renovation, however, for David Monteith, Helen Vance, Linda Hogue, and other descendants of those who lived on Hazel Creek and the North Shore, is the upstairs museum commemorating the history of the county and honoring their ancestors.

In April 2016, in frustration over Congressional inaction, the Swain County Board of Commissioners filed a lawsuit in the Court of Federal Claims in D.C. to force the government to pay the balance on the agreement. Commissioner Steve Moon argued to the *Smoky Mountain News*, "It's about our only option left. The federal government has actually lied to us for so many years—it's been 70 years since the original promise was made—very little has ever been done. They've made it seem like it's perfectly fine to lie to the citizens, so we need to try to hold them accountable." The D.C. law firm of Hogan Lovell filed the suit against the Department of Interior on the grounds of "failure to cooperate, breach of implied duty of good faith and fair dealing, and breach of contract." The complaint reads in part, "All the government's broken promises and foot-dragging for the better part of a century is a great injustice to the County's residents... NPS's [the National Park Service] failure even to request sufficient funds constitutes a breach of its contractual duty to cooperate in fulfilling the 2010 agreement." Ironically, Swain County will be using interest from the $12.8 million initial settlement payment to finance its suit.

Time will only tell if the federal government finally upholds its end of the bargain before the 2010 agreement expires in 2020. But for most Swain County residents, the road issue remains a thorn in their side and the inaction on the part of the federal government has simply maintained the truth of a sign posted prominently on the Road to Nowhere just outside the park boundary boldly asserting:

WELCOME TO
THE ROAD TO NOWHERE
A BROKEN PROMISE
1943 - ?

The Road to Nowhere

THE "ROAD TO NOWHERE" CULMINATES IN THIS 1,200-FOOT TUNNEL,
THE LAST WORK DONE ON THE ROAD WAS IN 1970. ONLY HIKERS, PARK
SERVICE VEHICLES, AND THE OCCASIONAL BEAR MAY PASS THROUGH IT.

*A*s I was nearing completion of this book in early August 2015, I returned to Hazel Creek with my brother David and UNC Asheville colleague Evan Gurney. The two-hour drive to the Cable Cove boat ramp and the one-hour paddle across the lake to Proctor reminded me of the ongoing challenges of getting to Hazel Creek. It is still not easy. As I walked along what was once known as Calico Street and up the trail past the ruins of the Ritter Lumber Co. mill I reflected on the things I have learned while writing this book and trying to "get to" the meaning of the place. I was struck by how much things have changed here in the past 100 years. A place that not that long ago echoed with the sounds of busy woodhicks heading for work, women going about their shopping in the town stores, children playing on the school playground, folks singing hymns in the Proctor Baptist Church, of train whistles and screeching locomotive wheels, and the scream of band-saws as massive trees were cut into lumber, now echoes only with the eerie cries of pileated woodpeckers and the caws of crows.

Indeed, as we hiked up the trail the word that kept coming into my head was "solitude." In the eight hours or so we were in the area we saw only a couple of folks on horseback at the head of the trail, two backpackers heading down the trail to the lake to catch the shuttle, three more that passed us going up the trail as we fished, a couple of Park Service employees on an ATV, a couple in a tandem kayak glimpsed in the distance heading back across the lake as we came out, and the pilot of the shuttle and two backpackers being transported in as we prepared to cast off

Horace Kephart Memorial Boulder

THIS BOULDER OVERLOOKS BRYSON CITY.

our boats and head home. We saw no one else in the stream and our fishing went largely undisturbed, unfortunately not even by the fish, although I did get some strikes and actually caught a couple and David and Evan were able to pull in a few decent size fish, and a few miniscule ones.

In the midst of being lost in Hazel Creek's solitude, however, I was inescapably reminded of Hazel Creek's past. Invariably as I climbed in or out of the stream I came across some piece of metal that had some indeterminate use in those boom and bust years of the area's industrial past. We also passed a couple of boats moored near the head of the trail, an ATV, and a Hazel Creek buggy used by the National Park Service not only in day-to-day management activities but to help get descendants of those interred in area cemeteries up the creek for annual summer grave decorations.

But knowledge of Hazel Creek's past and the pieces of evidence of that past only made the solitude of the place more noticeable. As we paddled back across the lake we witnessed one of the most gorgeous sites one can imagine as the glassy-smooth lake reflected the mountains in the late afternoon light. Fortunately for the state of our friendship, Evan was dutifully impressed by his first experience on Hazel Creek and even tolerated all the stories I shared, gleaned from two years or so of being steeped in the history of the place. David is always happy to just fish and has to tolerate me and my stories because he is my brother. It was, however, in my estimation, a wonderful day and a powerful reminder of the lure and magic of Hazel Creek.

The next day I had the privilege of returning to Swain County and sitting and talking with local historian Don Casada. Don has probably walked more of the Hazel Creek watershed in the last few years than anyone alive and has identified and visited almost every homesite located on the North Shore. Indeed, Granville

Calhoun and his bear hunting buddies are probably the only people who walked more of the area. We ended the day with a walk through the Bryson City Cemetery with Don pointing out the graves of significant individuals in Swain County history. Most interesting for me were those of folks who had strong Hazel Creek connections, a poignant reminder of all the people who helped make this a special and unique place.

The most prominent grave in the cemetery is that of Horace Kephart, located front and center and marked by a large boulder. His monument reminds us of his ongoing legacy in using the people of Hazel Creek to characterize life and culture in the Southern Appalachian region. That legacy still sparks controversy, despite his obvious affection and respect for his neighbors, and is one that forms the unfortunate basis for many a cable channel reality show. Not far from Kephart's grave are the graves of land speculator and Bone Valley resident John E. Coburn and Ritter Lumber Co. chief civil engineer Orson Burlingame and his wife, Forney Creek native Lillie Lucille Brooks Burlingame, reminders of the transformation of Hazel Creek by industrial forces in the late 19th and early 20th century.

James Holland "Hol" Rose, who figured prominently in one chapter of *Our Southern Highlanders* and whose life and death helped reinforce some of those stereotypical images is buried just over the hill. A nephew of moonshining legend Quill Rose, Hol, who evidently had experience making "shine" himself in his early days, became a Deputy Federal Prohibition Enforcement Agent, and a very zealous one, after ratification of the 18th Amendment. On October 25, 1920, J. E. "Babe" Burnette, who Rose was trying to arrest for making apple brandy, killed the agent in a shootout.

Near the back of the cemetery Don pointed out the grave of legendary fisherman/bear hunter Mark Cathey, a reminder of the historic significance of those activities on Hazel Creek from the arrival of the first Native Americans to 1944, and in the case of fly fishing, up to the present day. Cathey has what must be the most interesting epitaph in the cemetery, one that emphasizes the importance of evangelical Christianity in the region: "Beloved hunter and fisherman was himself caught by the gospel hook just before the season closed for good."

I was most gratified to be able to pay my respects to Granville Calhoun whose grave lies in a far corner of the cemetery. Calhoun lived on Hazel Creek for 58 of his 104 years and played at least some role in every important juncture in the community's history from the 1890s up to his removal in 1944. He perhaps best represents the qualities that make the individuals who lived on Hazel Creek much more than Appalachian stereotypes. While his image as a tough and rugged, yarn-spinning bear hunter may fit such stereotypes, his intelligence, ingenuity, entrepreneurship, creativity, community spirit, and support for education and modernization make him emblematic of the reality of life on Hazel Creek.

All of the memories of this community are not interred in the Bryson City

Cemetery or the ones scattered throughout the Hazel Creek watershed. Those memories are kept alive by the ever dwindling numbers of individuals who lived there as young adults or children who still make the trek to cemetery decorations and annual reunions and who continue to work to preserve the area's rich history. Of course, for many folks in Swain County and for descendants of those who lived on the North Shore scattered throughout the country, the painful memories of the long struggle to secure the future of those cemeteries and have the federal government honor its 1943 commitment to replace NC 288 will stay on their minds and, on occasions, will appear in media reports.

For the most part, however, Hazel Creek has stayed out of the news in recent years and is probably the quietest it has been in a long time. Hazel Creek did return to the headlines for a brief period in early June 2015, but in a way that probably ensured that even fewer visitors would make the long trek in. A 250-pound black bear attacked a 16-year old Ohio boy camping at a backcountry campsite near the confluence of Sugar Fork and Hazel Creek, grabbing him by the head and dragging him from his hammock. The boy's father fought off the bear, provided first aid, helped him down the trail 4.5 miles, woke some campers near the lake who had a boat, and transported him across the lake to the Cable Creek landing where emergency personnel transported him to the hospital. After a few days in the hospital the boy was able to go home to Ohio and appeared to have no permanent injuries. Park Service rangers captured and euthanized a bear after the attack. The incident stayed in the news for a few weeks until a subsequent spike in shark attacks and a deadly grizzly bear attack in Yellowstone National Park diverted the press's attention.

But despite the relative quiet and solitude of Hazel Creek today the place still deserves our attention and embodies some powerful lessons that will never lose their relevance. The fight by former residents to preserve the memory of Moses Proctor, Granville Calhoun, and countless others who called this watershed home reminds us, in a world of increasingly atomized and isolated individuals, of the power of community. Folks with ties to Hazel Creek still share a special bond and not just because of the fight to build the road.

At the same time, the fight over the Road to Nowhere contains some powerful lessons as well. It teaches us that "in order to form a more perfect union" the government needs to be held accountable and needs to fulfill its promises, something that resonates far beyond the banks of Hazel Creek. It also teaches us that determined and well-organized people can make a difference. The folks of the North Shore Cemetery Association and North Shore Historical Association may not have secured the road they desired into Hazel Creek, but they made sure the federal government was not able to forget it had made a solemn promise to Swain County. Until the debt to the county, and to the people of the North Shore, is finally paid off, and perhaps as long as people who once lived in the community still survive, the words Hazel Creek will be inextricably tied to the words "broken promise."

But ultimately, and in the long term, Hazel Creek represents not a broken promise, but the fulfillment of a promise by that same federal government to preserve some very special places, in the words of the Organic Act that created the National Park Service, "unimpaired for future generations." Hazel Creek qualifies as one of those special places on so many levels. Yes, it was anything but a wilderness for much of the 20th century. But the fact that this place was once a site of heavy industry, a semi-urban area, heavily scarred by destructive logging practices and now approaches old-growth forest status; was once a place whose streams ran full of silt and human waste and now teems with trout; and was once a place where wildlife habitat was virtually wiped out and now provides homes for a wide variety of forest creatures, including bears, speaks to that promise. Indeed, in a world where activists of all stripes preach the gospel of inevitable decline, of coming apocalypse, Hazel Creek represents a powerful message of redemption.

Selected Bibliography

Great Smoky Mountains Area History
Dunn, Durwood, *Cades Cove: The Life and Death of a Southern Appalachian Community,* 1818 - 1937
Holland, Lance, *Fontana: A Pocket History of Appalachia*
Jabbour, Alan & Karen, *Decoration Day in the Mountains*
Plott, Bob, *Colorful Characters of the Great Smoky Mountains*
Taylor, Stephen, *The New South's New Frontier*

Native Americans and Environment
Bartram, William, *Travels of William Bartram*
Hudson, Charles, *Southeastern Indians*
Keel, Bennie, *Cherokee Archaeology*
Mooney, James, *History, Myths, and Sacred Formulas of the Cherokees*
Silver, Timothy, *A New Face on the Countryside*

Logging History
Pierce, Daniel, *Logging in the Smokies*
Ritter Lumber Co., *The Hardwood Bark*
Schmidt, Ronald and William Hooks, *Whistle Over the Mountain*
Weals, Vic, *Last Train to Elkmont*

Hazel Creek History
Kephart, Horace, *Our Southern Highlanders*
Myers, Wendy, "Reflections of Olde Swain" Blog
(http://reflectionsofoldeswain.blogspot.com/)
Oliver, Duane, *Hazel Creek From Then Till Now*
. . . . . Along the River: People and Places
. . . . . Remembered Lives: A History of Our Family

Hunting and Fishing in the Smokies
Casada, Jim, *Fly Fishing in the Great Smoky Mountains National Park*
Gasque, Jim, *Hunting and Fishing in the Great Smokies*
Hunnicutt, Samuel, *Twenty Years of Hunting and Fishing in the Great Smoky Mountains*
Kirk, Don, *Smoky Mountains Trout Fishing Guide*
Middleton, Harry, *On the Spine of Time*
Plott, Bob, *A History of Hunting in the Great Smoky Mountains*

Moonshine
Dabney, Joseph, *Mountain Spirits*
Pierce, Daniel, *Corn From a Jar: Moonshining in the Great Smoky Mountains*
Stewart, Bruce, *Moonshiners and Prohibitionists*

*Page numbers followed by ph refer to photographs and their captions.